ROGER FR... T0314892

BITE SIZE
WORLD

EATING MY WAY AROUND THE PLANET

ROGER FRANKHAM

BITE SIZE
WORLD

EATING MY WAY AROUND THE PLANET

MEREO
Cirencester

Mereo Books

1A The Wool Market Dyer Street Cirencester Gloucestershire GL7 2PR
An imprint of Memoirs Publishing www.mereobooks.com

Bite Size World: 978-1-86151-184-3

First published in Great Britain in 2014
by Mereo Books, an imprint of Memoirs Publishing

The address for Memoirs Publishing Group Limited can be found at
www.memoirspublishing.com

Cover Design - Ray Lipscombe

Author photo - Avi Ohana

The Memoirs Publishing Group Ltd Reg. No. 7834348

The Memoirs Publishing Group supports both The Forest Stewardship Council® (FSC®)
and the PEFC® leading international forest-certification organisations. Our books carrying
both the FSC label and the PEFC® and are printed on FSC®-certified paper. FSC® is the
only forest-certification scheme supported by the leading environmental organisations
including Greenpeace. Our paper procurement policy can be found at
www.memoirspublishing.com/environment

Typeset in 9/14pt Franklin Gothic
by Wiltshire Associates Publisher Services Ltd. Printed and bound in Great Britain by
Printondemand-Worldwide, Peterborough PE2 6XD

CONTENTS

Acknowledgements
About the author
Dedication
Foreword

Part One – Australia & Asia

Part Two – Europe & North Africa

Part Three – North America

Appendix

ACKNOWLEDGMENTS

A big thank you to my editor, Chris Newton at Memoirs Books, Bonnie Britt and Dianne Jacob for their input and suggestions.

This book could not have been written without the assistance and support of the following people. This has come in many forms: a bed for the night, a homecooked meal or an invitation out to dinner, advice, feedback, recommendations, inspiration, transport, kitchens to experiment in, and so much more!

Thelma Abhyankar, Eddie Alcantar, Carole Alexander, Engin Akin, David Barnett, Maureen Bell, Sabrina Bolin, Jayna Boon, Haili Britton, Stuart Busby, Liz Button, Danny & Sally Cahalan, Lilia Cardenas, Gina Carpinito, Rod Coogan, Bianca Cook, Courtney Cook, Michael Coon, Robyn De Luca, Phyllis Dolgin, Robin Durham, John T Edge, Zoe Feigenbaum, Sonya Garibay, LeAnne Gault, Lynda Gerty, Hasan of Padang, Di Holuigue, Kirkland Hu, Stephen Hudson, Beryl Jackson, Nancy Harmon Jenkins, Erna Kaaber, Louise Kelaher, Anne Langdon, Alex & Jane Laskos, Ellen & Bob Laughland, Dave Legget, Sarah Legget, Dorothy & Michael Long, Maile Kop (who makes the best *Spam Musubi*!), Jada Li, Annette Lindsay, Peta Jane Lindsay, Richard Lindsay, Christine Manfield, Kathy & Doug Martinides, Andrew Maynard, Tommy & Cat McEwen, Tim & Jenny Murphy, Andrew Nicolson, Mariko Ono, Karen Ong, James Oseland, Danny Pegoraro, Des Peters, Kiran Prasad, Carol Puckett, Alan Richman, Simon Riik, David Rosengarten, Julie Sahni, Luisita 'Chit' Saunders, Tara Saysombath, Bill & Jenny Sheaffe, Kate & Christa Sheaffe, Anita Singh-Peters, Ian Smith (who came up with the book's title), James & Melissa Stephens, Renie Steves, Marilyn Tausend, Chris Taylor, Gavin Taylor, Carl Teece, Jerry Traunfeld, Gene Tu, Shirley Tu, Gwyn Vose, Kristy Williams and Mike Wilson.

And the Frankhams: David, Tomas, Reiley and Richard.

ABOUT THE AUTHOR

Roger Frankham graduated with straight As from the French Culinary Institute in New York and has lived and worked on four continents. This is his first book. **www.rogerfrankham.com**

For Helen, and all my family

FOREWORD

In the late nineties when I was living in Vancouver I played 'Spin the Globe' with some food-minded friends, including a couple of chefs. The idea behind the game was simple. One of the homes we would get together in had a large globe. You gave it a good whirl and then, eyes shut, stopped it with your finger. Wherever the finger had landed, it was your turn that month to host a dinner party with food from that country. (If it was open water you spun again, although I guess someone could have made an argument for *sashimi* - raw fish.)

I can't confirm there was any actual peeking, but one person did seem to land a lot on Italy, and Italian food was what he most liked to cook. On my first spin, I opened my eyes to find my finger resting on Saudi Arabia. I knew almost nothing about the country or its cuisine. I took on the challenge, learning as much as I could online and at the library. And then, unbelievably, I just happened that week to meet at work a family who were originally from Saudi Arabia! They were bewildered but helpful as I grilled them on their eating habits, and they even suggested where in town might be the one store that stocked preserved limes for the Saudi spice blend *kabsa*.

The dinner party went pretty well, although I don't know how accurate the food was as I still haven't been to Saudi Arabia. The months rolled around, and when it was next my turn I was hoping for an easier assignment. But it was Kazakhstan, involving numerous variations on the theme of mutton.

The game faded away as people lost interest or moved, but the idea remained with me that other than the usual suspects (Italian, French, Chinese), there was an entire world of food out there I knew little about.

Fast forward a few years, to late 2006 and I was living and working in Sydney, Australia. I was now into my thirties, currently single and without major commitments, some money in the bank and an itch to travel. What about a once-in-a-lifetime food trip around the planet? And with food as the central experience, not just within the context of encountering different cultures. I felt this was an opportunity I had to take. Who knew if I would ever get the chance of a journey like this again? I left my job and bought a plane ticket.

The plan was simple: find and eat some of the best food the world had to offer. That didn't have to mean the most expensive. I hoped it wouldn't, and as it turned out usually it wasn't. Over the next eight months and 23 countries, there were times when I took a bite of something so amazing that everything seemed to stop around me – whatever it was I was eating was all I could think about. They're all in here, of course, and so are the merely good, the disappointing, and the inedible, designed to shock and awe unsuspecting tourists (looking at you, Icelandic rotten shark).

This is a book about food, but it's not about important issues such as the lack in many places of it (some one in seven of the world's population go to bed hungry), or the politics of excess (one estimate says forty per cent of the food purchased in the US is wasted) or sustainability. I make my own private contributions towards tackling these matters. I was a witness to appalling poverty and hardship in my travels. I'm well aware just how incredibly lucky and privileged I was to be able to swan around the Earth stuffing my face. But rather than dwell on the distressing things I saw, I wanted this to be a more upbeat and narrow-focused account. Simply, one traveller's impressions of what he ate, and his discovery that something wonderful and positive *is* available around this mixed-up planet - the pleasures of the table offered up to us by generous, hospitable and hardworking cooks.

A few of the foods I came across are controversial. I tried to put my prejudices aside and enter into the spirit of each destination, and eat as a local would. Occasionally this meant trying things which, for one reason or other, I normally wouldn't.

This isn't an up-to-date travel guide. Restaurants have closed; chefs have moved on; food trends wax and wane. Whole neighbourhoods I've visited have gone - like the *hutongs*, the narrow alleys of Beijing, bulldozed out of existence before the Olympics. But it's a portrait of how, and what, at least part of Earth's population were eating at the start of the 21st century.

Some of what I saw and ate might disappear altogether in an increasingly globalized world and its generic cuisine. It's already possible to circumnavigate it without any change to your diet, if that's what you want to do. A lot of traditional recipes and techniques are labour intensive. They were developed when there was little alternative and short cuts simply weren't an option. Now, the convenience of fast and processed food is everywhere.

How many cooks will still insist on rolling out fresh noodles by hand, spend absurd numbers of hours assembling intricate sweets, or continue to pinch each dumpling together by hand for their meal, when frozen, pre-prepared versions are increasingly available? A compromise in taste and texture, yes, but a major time saver, and if they come to be consumed regularly instead of the original, the new and lower benchmark.

So here are snapshots of a changing world in the early years of this century, a world which, as you read this, no longer exists. All inaccuracies are mine. My perceptions aren't necessarily factual – just the way I saw things.

Travelling around the world, one will sometimes come across some interesting ways with English in places less used to speaking and writing it. ("Fried children" for chicken on one menu comes to mind.) I give a few examples throughout the book that caught my eye, but in no way are these meant to patronise or belittle. I have the greatest respect for anyone who can speak or write more than one language – something I can't do myself with any skill. I make enough mistakes with this one.

A NOTE ON THE RECIPES

Each chapter has a recipe. They mightn't be authentic to someone who is from that country, or who really knows and understands its food, and they don't try too hard to be. Plenty of cookbooks that are written by experts do a great job of that! Instead they are my own, very personal, take on what I encountered - my interpretation, filtered through my tastes and experiences.

A recipe is only a guideline. I've seen twenty-five cooks follow an identical recipe in the same kitchen and get completely different results. Your stove, your oven, your pots and pans are all factors (ovens especially can vary, and can be as much as a hundred degrees out from the temperature it says on the dial). Trust your senses as well as the written word. And if a recipe's not working out, get in touch and we'll put our heads together and try to figure it out!

INGREDIENTS

The recipes were made using large (50 gram) eggs, salted butter (you could use unsalted), and table or fine sea salt. For sugar I normally used a finer grain of white sugar, called caster/castor sugar in Australia and the UK, superfine sugar in the US and berry sugar in Canada.

By the way, if you're ever wondering why your food doesn't taste like restaurant food, the answer might be salt. It's jaw-dropping at times how much salt goes into something to make it "properly seasoned" to the chef. In each recipe I've suggested an amount which, in my opinion, is the minimum necessary to achieve a 'correct' taste.

The same ingredient can vary by name in different countries, which can be confusing. Sugar's an example mentioned above, and tomato paste would be called 'tomato puree' in the UK (while in the US 'tomato puree' would refer to a sauce). 'Thin' and 'light' soy sauce are more or less the same thing but don't mean low sodium, which is a different option.

Adding a bit of tomato paste to stews and sauces adds body, depth and colour without drawing too much attention to itself, and it's a lighter way to thicken them than flour or cream. Not all tomato pastes are created equal. They can be insipid; it goes back to the quality of the tomatoes used. The best I ever tasted was in Sicily - *estratto*, slow-dried in the sun and so delicious you can eat it straight out of the jar like jam. But I wouldn't know where to get it outside Sicily. Look instead for double or triple concentrated tomato paste. The Italian brand Mutti is the best brand widely available – it comes in a toothpaste-like tube or a small can and I've seen it in stores in the UK, US and Australia.

Other name brand products I use and prefer in the recipes:

Light soy sauce – Pearl River Bridge Superior Light
Dark soy sauce – Pearl River Bridge Superior Dark
Mushroom soy sauce – Pearl River Bridge Mushroom Flavoured Superior Dark Soy
Japanese soy sauce – Kikkoman
Oyster sauce – Lee Kum Kee Premium
Maggi Seasoning
Spring roll wrappers – TYJ brand
Chinese sausage – Wing Wing
Stone's Green Ginger Wine
Aalborg Akvavit
Vodka - Polmos Bialystok Zubrówka (Bison Grass Vodka)

MEASUREMENTS

I use the US and UK tablespoon measurement, which is equivalent to 3 teaspoons or 15 ml (*not* the Australian tablespoon, which is 4 teaspoons or 20 ml).

Conversions between metric and volume are not always exact and may be rounded up or down. If I haven't been exact in a recipe it's because either amount will work.

DIRECTIONS

'Cooking Time' is actual time cooking and doesn't include your preparation time spent chopping up ingredients and opening cans and bottles, or rereading the recipe and cursing me for not being clearer.

Cooking times can vary enormously, depending on the equipment and the kitchen. I have often been vague in these recipes about cooking times as I don't find an instruction such as "cook onions for 5 minutes" very helpful. It's meant to be helpful, in giving you an idea, but it may be way off and doesn't tell you what you are trying to achieve. Where possible I have instead indicated the result you are going for – "cook onions until golden brown" – however long that may take.

Making the roux for the Etouffee (p 195) took me 10 minutes on a gas range in Vancouver and 45 minutes on an electric hot plate in a London bedsit. After an hour in a friend's oven in Melbourne, my Lemon Delicious (p 9) was completely raw. After the same time in an LA friend's oven it was burnt to a crisp. So please use any times stated in the recipes as a guideline only.

Most recipes are to serve four people - so double for eight, halve for two, and quarter for one (or make as is, and get a few meals out of it).

EQUIPMENT

I consider heavy-bottomed pots and pans to be essential equipment if you don't want your food to stick and burn. A Microplane rasp is a brilliant tool for grating ingredients like ginger and garlic straight into the pot whenever a recipe calls for 'finely chopped' or 'minced'.

COOKING AHEAD

One recurring theme of these recipes could be described as 'stews around the world'. It's a popular and economical cooking method. *Menudo, rendang, etouffee, dal, imam bayildi* – all are essentially stews; meat and/or vegetables cooked in liquid. A stew will benefit from being made, refrigerated overnight, and reheated to serve. The improvement in flavour can be dramatic. Something like a curry can taste a bit confused when it's first cooked, all the spices jangling, but after a day in the fridge it has mellowed into a sustained note of one savoury flavour. So if you can, consider making anything that is braised or stewed a day ahead.

PART ONE
AUSTRALIA & ASIA

AUSTRALIA

When my grandfather was in his eighties and living alone, my mother decided to try to improve his diet. It consisted mostly of meat, bread, cheese and fruit - not a lot of vegetables (although he would have room for sweets). Even the smell of onions cooking might bring a suspicious "Is that garlic?"

She bought him a grill, to stop him from frying all his meals. He went along with the scheme and cooked some sausages on the new gadget, the fat from the plump bangers seeping out and falling away in sizzling splashes to coat the pan underneath the grill.

"Ooh, look at all that lovely grease" thought Granddad, and fried his eggs in the bottom of the tray.

. . . .

The meat-and-potatoes Australia he grew up in still exists, although these days even far-flung rural towns might have a Thai restaurant or two. Sydney, Australia's largest city, home to a fifth of its population, has changed radically over the years. What had been a mainly-white outpost of distant Britain has now become extremely multicultural, quite Asian in parts. Its nascent culinary scene surges forward, excited by new spices and unfamiliar ingredients. TV cooking shows flood the airwaves. Glossy, don't-really-try-this-at-home chef cookbooks fly off the shelves.

To eat in Sydney today is the tale of a city, told through its food: A late-night pie with peas and gravy at Harry's Café De Wheels: the meat pie is *the* iconic Aussie foodstuff, and a true pie-lover will at some point make the pilgrimage to Harry's food cart, open for business since 1945. There might be better-rated pies in town these days, but every bite of Harry's is historic. Beneath the "tiger" pie's wan pastry crust are hearty chunks of beef, with plenty of black pepper.

A bowl of spaghetti in No Names, an unsigned cafeteria above an inner city pool hall. No Names has served up cheap plates of pasta to starving students and local workers for over fifty years. It took me ten of those years to get the recipe for their sauce out of the Italian expat who runs it, but, as it turns out, making it in your own kitchen isn't the same as walking upstairs into No Names.

Breakfasts of yoghurt laced with fresh passion fruit, or buttered crumpets slathered with the black goo Vegemite (a yeasty brewery by-product).

Weekend trolleys of *yum cha* (*dim sum*) in Chinatown. Grilled seafood brunches in the cafes of Bondi Beach. Sausage rolls at the Bourke Street Bakery, and freshly baked Turkish bread at the corner of Cleveland and Crown in Surry Hills. These are some of the quintessential tastes of Sydney, beloved by thousands of its residents.

· · · · · · · · · ·

Behind the food are major global events, triggering waves of immigration that changed Australian eating forever. The original Aboriginal inhabitants were followed by British settlers in the late 18th century and the arrival of Chinese labourers for the Gold Rush a hundred years later. After the Second World War came populations of Greeks and Italians, and later Vietnamese and Thai.

At city bakeries you can start the day with a bacon and egg roll (Australians love bacon and eggs - it's even a pizza topping) or perhaps a 'finger bun', a sweet yellow roll hiding an occasional raisin within and iced with a stripe of pink fondant. I have no idea how the finger bun got its name, but maybe it won't matter for too much longer. They are becoming harder to find, muscled out by more international breakfast treats like muffins.

In Sydney's central business district and its suburban malls, workers take their lunch breaks at the food courts. Noodles are slurped. Pies are squirted with Sauce (more on Sauce later). Green, yellow and red curries are ladled over plastic containers of rice, and customers upsold to larger containers – if they were to look closely, it's the same amount of curry with an additional heaping of rice. The more restrained or waistline-conscious pick at salad sandwiches stained crimson with beetroot.

After work, or instead of work - or even, sometimes, during work! - Australians put away a lot of beer. Drinking venues like the pub, the RSL (Returned Services League) and sporting club also offer hot meals. Traditionally this would be steak-with-chips fare, but now is just as likely to be Chinese or South-East Asian.

The 'milk bar' is a local institution, difficult to define to someone who hasn't been to one but something of a cross between a convenience store and a diner. You can drop in for a hamburger or greasy fish and chips – and I do mean greasy, their cooking oil is never hot enough - or order deep-fried "scallops" made of mashed potato and sprinkled with 'chicken salt' (essentially crumbled bouillon cube). Or you can just pick up a loaf of bread to go - and there's milk for sale too, of course.

An Aussie Milk Bar Hamburger, fully loaded, has - in addition to bun and patty - grilled onion, bacon, fried egg (there's that bacon and egg again) and a pineapple ring, with beetroot (there's that beetroot again) standing in for the dill pickle they use in the US (Australian teenagers were once notorious for wallpapering McDonalds outlets with discarded slices of dill pickle). Visiting Americans can be astonished by this combination, especially when the beetroot mingles with the meat juices to make it seem like you're eating an alarmingly rare burger.

And the burger must have Sauce. When Australians talk about Sauce, there's none of that French fuss of hundreds of codified variations. In Australia, Sauce means one thing, and that is the local version of tomato ketchup. (Connoisseurs do insist on a difference between ketchup and Sauce - Sauce is slightly less sweet.) Barbecue Sauce is the alternative to Sauce; a little more vinegary and brown, rather than red.

Sauce sorted, a crash course in Aussie Lingo might help the uninitiated with more of the local food – or should I say, *tucker*.

Chook: chicken.

A *snag* is a sausage, that might be cooked on a *barbie* – barbecue grill. Slap white bread around the sausage, with Sauce of course, and you have a *sanger*, a sandwich.

To drink, *grog*: alcohol, which might take the form of *plonk* (wine) or *a tinnie* (a can of beer).

Or how about a *bickie* – a biscuit, i.e. cookie? Have one along with a *cuppa* – a cup of tea – or a *flat white*, hot coffee with milk.

Since the 1980s, Thai has become the default ethnic cuisine, the way Indian is in the UK or Mexican in parts of the US. Some of the best Thai food outside Thailand is in Sydney and Melbourne. But really you can take your pick of the world's foods here - from Chinese dumplings for breakfast to late-night drinkers steadying their bellies with *doner* kebabs (meat roasted on a vertical rotating spit) brought to these shores by Turkish and Lebanese migrants.

··········

Is there a true national cuisine, though? A few years ago indignant headlines reported that two Australian cooks had been denied work visas for Japan. The customs inspectors had never heard of

"Australian cuisine", and so couldn't class the visitors as experts in their field.

Sydney's celebrity chefs leapt to their nation's defence, citing the cerebral creations served in their restaurants. Still, maybe because in its current incarnation it's such a young country, barely 200 years old, Australia is atypical in that hardly any of the native flora and fauna are used in its cooking. Some fish and seafood is. Once in a while marketing pushes promote kangaroo meat, but the percentage of people that eat it is low (perhaps the memory of cute TV pet 'Skippy the Bush Kangaroo' lingers). In the average Australian household kitchen on a given day, I suspect there wouldn't be a single ingredient that is native. All the local animals, fruit and vegetables, spices and herbs, are largely ignored.

An indigenous fare does exist - the traditional diet of the Aborigines who were in Australia for forty thousand years or more before white settlers. The Aborigines lived off the land, hunting wallaby with spears and boomerangs, wrapping fish in treebark to be baked in earthen pits, gathering roots and grubs. Today though, ninety percent of Australia's population live in cities, where the ingredients and techniques of 'bush tucker' are unknown. Recently, allied with the global trend towards culinary localism, some Australian chefs and delicatessens are starting to feature native foods. In time this should have an influence on the home cook.

· · · · · · · · · ·

The confectionery in Australia is among the best in the world, British-inspired and made with quality ingredients: real chocolate, real butter and vanilla, actual sugar instead of cheaper corn syrup. The most famous treat is the *Tim Tam*, two chocolate *bickies* sandwiching a chocolatey caramel cream and coated in milk chocolate. The *Mint Slice* is not as well known outside the country but is even better, essentially the same concept but with the chocolate flavour in the filling replaced by peppermint oil - like eating a cookie while brushing your teeth. The *Golden Gaytime* gets a chuckle from tourists at its name, but earns respect when they take a bite of the combination of honeycomb ice cream dipped in chocolate and *bickie* crumbs. Another frozen confection, the Splice, is a shell of lime-spiked pineapple sorbet around a core of vanilla ice cream.

Lamingtons, squares of pound cake rolled in melted chocolate and coconut, are an Australian classic, although if you want to start an argument – sorry, discussion - ask an Australian and a New Zealander just which country invented them.

· · · · · · · · · ·

Today is Shrove Tuesday - International Pancake Day. It's the first time in a few years that I've remembered the date, and I decide to go all out in celebrating it. In the morning I make a French crêpe with lemon and sugar, and - modifying the same batter - a thicker American-style pancake topped with butter and golden syrup. At lunchtime I'm in an Indian café in Cleveland Street tucking into *masala dosa*, a large, paper-thin Indian crêpe filled with curried potato. Dinner starts with a couple of Peking Duck pancakes, drizzled in hoisin sauce, from Chinatown's BBQ King. It's a short walk from there to the Little Korea around Pitt Street, where I pick up a *kimchi* pancake pockmarked with little green onions.

In a Vietnamese restaurant in Surry Hills I order *banh xeo*, a yellow rice flour crêpe folded around roasted pork, bean sprouts and a fistful of fresh herbs. Finally, late at night for dessert I whip up Austrian *palatschinken,* spread with apricot preserves. Pancake Day is over and it's a good thing too, because right now it feels like it's going to be several years before I want to see another one. Pancakes from seven countries in one day, and all within a few city blocks. Sydney is one of the few cities in the world where this would be possible.

·· · · · · · · · ·

"It's a big responsibility to feed somebody" muses Anna Heifetz. "To restore them, make them feel better, see them enjoying it."

She feeds people at Flying Taco on North Perth's Angove Street. Perth is the other side of the country from Sydney, and Flying Taco is possibly the city's first purveyor of truly Mexican street fare. Located in an old Italian neighbourhood, the shop is sandwiched between a café and a furniture store. The logo, a winged taco, is inspired by a tattoo which the illustrated Anna and her brother both wear. Ethnic touches inside are restrained - a few pieces of art, the odd sombrero, Latin music issuing at moderate volume from the stereo. A help-yourself fridge in one corner holds Brazilian and El Salvadorean sodas as well as the usual big-name suspects. The plastic chairs are orange, white and green.

Until recently, Latin American food has never been one of Australia's strengths. A friend worked at a Mexican restaurant in the 1980s.

"Look at the plate, mate," said the owner-chef, who had never set foot anywhere near Mexico. "You see green salad and avocado, red tomatoes and white sour cream as the Mexican flag. With the yellow tacos and brown beans, the colours are what's important. Doesn't matter what it tastes like. If it looks good, punters will like it."

Flying Taco, though, isn't one of the nacho and margarita joints lining James Street's rowdy thoroughfare downtown. Anna is on a separate mission. Her menu recreates the flavours she knew growing up in Los Angeles, where Latin food is as everyday as Thai cuisine is now to Australians. It's informed by her travels throughout Mexico, including time studying with renowned chefs Roberto Santibanez and Rick Bayless. After travelling across Asia Anna ended up under the cloudless blue skies of Western Australia, fell for the place, and after working in some local restaurants decided it "just felt right" to make her vision a reality here.

On a bright, light Friday afternoon Anna and one assistant move between the open kitchen and the counter facing the dining room, taking requests, delivering food-laden baskets to the handful of tables and disappearing behind sheets of flame as another order hits the griddle. Customers are young - singles or couples or young families - sporting piercings and body art.

"It's the tip of the iceberg," Anna says of her brief menu, unchanged since opening day except for occasional specials such as duck in sweet and sour *adobo*. One challenge for her is the local perceptions of Mexican food, created by the more widespread Americanised version.

Hard-shelled tacos, popular in the rest of the world, aren't that known in Mexico. Visitors to Flying Taco have been known to be taken aback by the real deal - warm rounds of soft corn tortillas patted out fresh from *masa harina* (lime-treated cornmeal), filled with a few mouthfuls of marinated grilled meat or stewed vegetable. A cup of one of a trio of house-made salsas comes alongside to splash on to taste at the diner's discretion. The green salsa is tangy with the sour green fruit called tomatillo, and the red one infused with the subdued, smoky heat of dried *chipotle* chilli. *Pico de Gallo* - "rooster's beak" – salsa hums with the freshness of ripe diced tomato folded through onion and coriander.

The taco fillings are a greatest hits of south of the border hole-in-the-walls and include *carne asada* and *pescado*, steak or fish steeped in spice and herbs before being cooked to order. In Mexico, *carnitas* is slabs of pork slow fried in huge vats of bubbling lard. In Perth, where good lard is harder to come by and frowned upon nutritionally, Anna achieves a similar effect by covering cubes of fresh pork with water and simmering the mixture down into a moist mass of shredded meat and concentrated cooking juices. Fresh pineapple, added to the taco, slices through the fattiness of the pig.

Substantial *burritos* have the same fillings as the tacos but are bulked out with rice and beans, a more American than Mexican conceit. The steak burrito is the store's biggest seller. Quesadillas, Latin toasted cheese sandwiches, are almost as popular. If you miss the crunch in the taco then go for the freshly-baked tortilla chips - some customers place an order just for those. Sourcing ingredients can be difficult in the world's most isolated city, but the situation is improving and regulars even help out. One drops by with the news that fresh jalapeño chillies have surfaced at the local supermarket.

Interest has been expressed in expanding the brand and taking it national, but Anna is in no rush. She's happy to stay small for now on Angove Street, gradually educating the public on the true tastes of a country and building a client base of loyal, happy eaters. It's fast food, yes, but made with quality ingredients and painstaking care. And something more, even.

The unsentimental Anna concurs. "There *is* a bit of love in the food."

LEMON DELICIOUS

Lemon Delicious is the most Australian of desserts to me, although it's not uniquely Aussie and appears in old British and American cookbooks. It's a family pudding. My grandmother and her generation of Australian country women made it. My mother made it. My aunt Jenny still makes it. It is a classic.

French chefs bang on about their lemon tarts as the ideal ending to a meal because they are so light. As the last recipe I remember for a lemon tart called for nine eggs, a quarter-litre of double cream and about two cups each of butter and sugar, clearly "light" is a relative term.

I love lemon tart! But Lemon Delicious is made up of the same flavours and ingredients and really *is* light. It's the perfect finish to a rich repast. As it bakes, the pudding separates into an airy, soufflé-like sponge cake atop a lemon custard. A tangy, fragrant dessert that combines elements of cake, sponge, soufflé and custard? Try it!

A Microplane is the handiest tool to extract zest (the thinnest part of the colored peel only) from a lemon. If doubling this recipe, use only 500 ml (2 cups) of milk.

Serves 4. Approximate cooking time: 60 minutes

1½ tablespoons (15 g) butter, plus additional butter to
grease the baking dish

½ cup (100 g) caster (superfine) sugar

3 tablespoons (45 ml) lemon juice (juice of 1-1½ lemons)

2 teaspoons finely grated lemon zest (from an
organic or unwaxed lemon)

2 large eggs, yolks and whites separated

1½ tablespoons (15 g) flour

1¼ cups (300 ml) whole milk

Preheat oven to 160 C (320 F). Lightly grease a 1 litre (4 cup) baking dish with butter.

Reserve 1 tablespoon of sugar. Place the butter and sugar in a large bowl and beat with an electric mixer until light and fluffy. (Or, soften butter to room temperature and beat by hand with a wooden spoon.) Add the lemon juice and zest. Add the egg yolks and beat until smooth. Add the flour and then the milk and beat briefly until the batter is smooth.

In a separate large bowl, whisk the egg whites to soft peaks. Add the remaining tablespoon of sugar and keep whisking until the peaks are firm. Gently fold the beaten egg whites into the lemon mixture. Pour the batter into the baking dish.

Pull the rack halfway out of the oven. Place a larger roasting pan on the rack, and then set a folded tea towel (dish cloth) inside it. Place the baking dish on the tea towel. Pour in hot water to halfway up the sides of the baking dish. (Called a water bath, or *bain marie*, this helps protect delicate custards from overcooking in the oven and scrambling.)

Place in the oven until the top is set and lightly browned, about

45–60 minutes. Carefully remove from oven. Remove baking dish from the hot water bath, and let stand 10 minutes before serving.

THE PHILIPPINES

Manila doesn't seem a place to care much for on first acquaintance. Initial impressions are of a city that is overcrowded, polluted and hot. The Philippines are largely off the backpacker circuit. The seven thousand islands that make up the rest of the country sound scenic, but right now a typhoon is hitting up the north and ongoing terrorism is flaring in the south, so it will be Manila only for this trip.

As with most big Asian cities, the roads are completely crazy and not for the faint-of-heart. Lanes, stoplights and even direction of traffic all appear to be optional. Some local sixth sense keeps things going more or less without incident, helped by the car horns which are the most important tool and in constant use. Luckily the drivers can't go too fast. Too many other cars, bikes, rickshaws, *jeepneys* (overcrowded minivans descended from US military vehicles) and pedestrians are blocking the way.

Airport-style metal detectors or staff waving security wands are at the entrances of all the shopping centres and major hotels. Guards outside retail stores carry automatic rifles. Even the Starbucks coffee shop has an armed guard standing by the door. Foreigners get waved through most places (I'm patted down entering a department store) while the locals get the brunt of the scrutiny. Signs at restaurants and bars read "Please Check Your Weapons In".

It's unclear whether this is a regular state of affairs or if recent incidents have ratcheted tensions higher than usual. The Philippines has always seen strife. At varying periods it has battled the Spanish, Japanese and US for independence, while finding time also to clash with China and Britain. Of late, local issues of corruption, rigged polls, assassinations and fundamentalist terrorism have kept the headlines busy. Ah, humanity!

It's a predominantly Catholic country, whose inhabitants take their religion seriously. Inscribed everywhere on taxis, *jeepneys* and storefronts:

"God IS Watching."

"Our Eternal Mother."

"Lord Save Us".

At a clothing shop at the mall the checkout girl writes "God Bless Our Sales" on my receipt.

Why come then to this city, so malodorous and congested with some twelve million people? Tourists who do trickle in, intimidated by the look of the local dives, may seek sustenance in the sterile safety of fast food chains. They are missing out on one truly good reason to visit Manila - Filipino food.

Outside Asia, hungry residents of other countries get their fix of South East Asian food primarily through Thai cuisine. Its supremacy is being challenged lately; Malaysian and Singaporean restaurants are on the rise, and Vietnamese is coming up through the ranks. But Pinoy (Filipino) cooking hasn't caught on as much yet.

It's a melting pot, an intrigue of Malay, Chinese, European and even Mexican influences (Mexico also a former colony of Spain). To a degree it seems fairly accessible - not overly spicy as some Asian fare can be, nor as challenging in texture as some of the more authentic Chinese preparations. It has savoury stews and vibrant stir fries, although some will be put off by what might be called Six Degrees of Sourness. The abundant use of vinegar in many dishes originated as a preserving technique, but is now embraced for its astringency. *Calamansi* is the other common souring agent, seen everywhere, a small citrus fruit like a lime crossed with a mandarin.

··········

I walk past a salon called "Be Beautiful for Him" on my way to lunch at Kamayan, a restaurant on my list from my pre-trip research. It's raining heavily and very hot. Despite carefully looking at a map before setting out, I'm now completely lost. This is not unusual. It is, however, a sign of progress that after several miles of walking I'm prepared this time to admit it.

Hailing a passing cab, I slump into the air-conditioned seat to find I've been heading in completely the wrong direction. We turn around as I chat with the driver.

"Things are so tough right now" says Cris, to my question about the economy. "My wife works in Saudi Arabia. I have no idea when I'll see her again. I really don't know. My son is four years old. He lives with his grandmother."

Time to change the subject. Both sports fans, we discuss the next match up for boxer Manny Pacquiao, national star of the Philippines. Cris is convinced he'll win easily. I'm not so sure, but mindful I'm in the car of a fervent supporter and remembering everyone around here seems to carry a gun, I claim to be neutral.

Kamayan turns out to be a buffet in the middle of a large mall, with a parade of greasy, congealed dishes and even the rice tasting tired. More of interest, in fact, is the menu at the adjacent McDonalds, where a "Rice Burger" has the usual bun component replaced by two compressed discs of cooked rice, speckled with black sesame seeds.

(Fast food is omnipresent here. All around the city are the usual McDonalds, KFC and Pizza Hut, but one of the most popular chains is Kenny Rogers' Roasters. Yes, that Kenny, the bearded country gent last seen knowing when to hold 'em and when to fold 'em. He now appears to be holding 'em in the chicken business and doing a roaring trade, in Manila at least.)

These first tastes don't have me in thrall, but things pick up when I head downstairs to the mall's food court with its myriad of vendors. Lots of dishes are displayed: *Kalderate* is hunks of beef with peppers, potatoes and green peas in a smooth tomato sauce. Swap beef for pork, and the dish is now called *menudo*. Fried rice contains "sizzling *sisig*", finely chopped pigs head. Plenty of vegetable dishes - *liang* are taro leaves softened in spiced coconut milk, and *sinigang* assorted native vegetables in a soup made sour with tamarind.

If there is a national dish, it must be *adobo* - meat (often chicken and pork together) marinated and then braised in soy sauce, vinegar, garlic, pepper and bay. The tangy version I try doesn't disappoint, although my still-squeamish sensibilities have me picking out and discarding the more generous lumps of pig fat. Over the next few days *adobo* will reappear as a filling for tiny spring rolls, on top of a pizza base paired uncomfortably with a lake of melted cheese, and as "*adobo* flakes' - the cooked meat shredded off the bone and crisped in a pan.

By late afternoon my guts are gurgling in protest at the introduction of so many new foods, and strongly suggesting I'm done for the rest of the day. I walk back to the hotel - carefully.

In the morning I eat at a street stall; a shack with a few tables beside a busy corner in a run-down part of town. No menu is posted, but pots of pre-prepared food simmer away, ready for the local workers. I ask if they have *bulalo*, beef shank soup. A bowl of clear broth is slid in front of me, bobbing in it a couple of morsels of gelatinous meat and some leafy greens. On a side plate is the ever-present *calamansi* fruit to add a souring squeeze or ten.

The broth is as deep and full-flavoured as a French consommé would be in some white-linen establishment. As I sip it I'm openly stared at - the odd person out - and the lady running the stall becomes quite protective. She hovers nearby, refilling my bowl a couple of times, showing me the right procedure for how and when to add the *calamansi*.

· · · · · · · · · ·

Over the following days I wander the streets of the city, grazing. One morning is spent in the upmarket Global City district, where expatriates mill about Australian coffee stores and European boutiques. Later, La Loma district on the other side of Manila is *lechon* country. Street after street is lined with row upon row of pigs spit-roasted over charcoal, ready to be purchased whole or by the kilo. Plastic bags contain *lechon* sauce, a grainy paste made from the livers.

Cabalen's lunch buffet provides a much better experience than Kamayan's. The Filipino names for many of the dishes remain a mystery, but they include a very sour soup with herbs; a fish broth strongly infused with ginger; the fried spring rolls, *lumpia*; glass noodles made from mung bean; oxtails and tripe in peanut sauce; organ meats bathed in inkly-black blood; pork liver in vinegar; leaves deep-fried in a tempura-like batter and a kind of paella, made of sticky rice.

Dinner at nearby Bistro Remedios is cooking from the Pampanga region of the country. Deep-fried whole frogs are stuffed with pork and spices. Swamp cabbage is sautéed with black beans and cubes of pork belly. A screwpine jelly, bright green, comes with buffalo milk ice cream and scrapings of young coconut.

....

Desserts in the Philippines are based, as they are in much of this part of the world, on sticky rice and coconut. *Palitaw ube* is a glutinous rice cake filled with *ube*, purple yam, and covered with powdered coconut (*ube* is a popular flavouring here, especially as a violet-hued ice cream). I come across another indigenous citrus, *dalandan*, this one larger than *calamansi* and resembling a green-skinned orange. It makes a great blended fruit shake.

Desserts that aren't rice-and-coconut based tend towards something like *halo halo*, a tall glass filled with milk, shaved ice, red beans and cubes of flan. Before trying it I think it's not really my thing. After trying it, I know it isn't. Beans for dessert? More to my liking is *suman*, another type of rice cake, steamed inside banana leaves to a gluey goodness and decorated with ripe mango.

Of all the assaults of tastes in Manila, the one that lingers most comes on a drizzly night at a place selling *bacolod inasal*, chicken grilled in the fashion of Negros province. The pieces of poultry are marinated in both *calamansi* juice *and* vinegar and grilled on bamboo skewers, then served with a sour - vinegar based, of course! - dipping sauce. When it's time for the acidity so avidly pursued by Filipino cooks, clearly it is Go Big or go home.

....

Slow Food is an organisation that began in Italy in the late eighties. Now it has branches (*convivia*) and thousands of members all over the world - the ultimate foodie gang. It's dedicated to preserving regional and traditional food preparations from the encroach of modernity and globalization. Maria Pardo de Tavera of the Manila chapter has invited me to a fundraising dinner at the Rockwell Club, a restaurant owned by a Slow Food member. Rockwell is another area for expats and wealthy Manilans with extensive security, high rise apartments and air-conditioned malls stocked with international brand stores.

"We focus on Filipino rice," Maria tells me. "The proceeds from the dinner are to send a grower to Italy at the end of the month for Terra Madre." She is referring to Slow Food's biannual international gathering in Turin, Italy of small scale farmers and food producers.

Different varieties of rice feature in each of the seven courses - as crackers topped with a salty, pungent pickle; as a side with roasted suckling pig, and turned into assorted desserts. *Sinigang* soup makes an appearance again, this time with *bangus* (milkfish), young coconut juice and *calamansi*. A salad of *alugbati* - malabar spinach - is seasoned with shrimp paste.

At the next table to us sits local celebrity cook "Chef Ed", a man of impressive girth and appetite. He's responsible for the suckling pig on tonight's menu. Although he is in jolly hail-fellow-well-met mode, when the pig is ready to be served you see in the glances he shoots his underlings that he is a perfectionist, and like many top chefs, probably not the easiest man to work for.

"His life is all about food," someone remarks of Chef Ed. Honestly, who can understand people who are obsessed like that?

Wait.

MENUDO (FILIPINO PORK STEW)

In Mexico *menudo* is a tripe soup, the default hangover cure, but in the Philippines the term refers to this meat and vegetable stew. For a funkier flavor, you could substitute a third or so of the pork with cubed pigs' liver. Serve with steamed rice.

'Light" soy sauce does not mean low sodium, but refers to the colour and texture, as opposed to "dark" soy (which is thicker and sweeter).

Serves 4. Approximate cooking time: 1 hour, 20 minutes

1 tablespoon lard or vegetable oil

450 g (1 pound) stewing pork, cut into 1 cm (½ inch) cubes

1 medium onion, finely chopped

1 medium carrot, cut into small dice

2 small garlic cloves, finely chopped

2 tomatoes, cut into small dice

1 red capsicum (bell pepper), de-seeded, cored
and cut into small dice

2 tablespoons tomato paste

2 tablespoons red wine vinegar

2 tablespoons light soy sauce

1 bay leaf

½ cup (125 ml) water or chicken stock (see appendix)

2 medium-sized waxy potatoes, peeled and cut into medium dice

½ cup frozen green peas

Heat the oil in a medium heavy-bottomed saucepan over medium-high heat. Brown the pork pieces all over, working in batches to avoid crowding the pan – if that happens they will steam instead of brown. Remove the pork to a plate. Leave the fat in the pan.

Add the onion and carrot to the pan, lower the heat to medium and cook until softened and the onion is translucent. Add the garlic, tomatoes and capsicum and cook for 2 minutes.

Add the tomato paste and fry for 2 minutes, stirring. Add the vinegar, soy, bay leaf and water or stock.

Return the pork and any juices that have accumulated to the pot. Bring to a boil over high heat, and then reduce heat to low. Simmer, partially covered, until the meat is almost tender, 30-40 minutes. Add the potatoes and continue cooking for another 15 minutes to cook them, then add the peas and cook for an additional 5 minutes.

MALAYSIA, SINGAPORE & INDONESIA

By sundown in the town of Kota Kinabalu, in Sabah in northern Borneo, any action is pretty much over and most of the shops and eateries closed. This is the Malaysian part of an island divided up with Indonesia and Brunei. Located near Mount Kinabalu, one of Asia's highest peaks, KK is smaller, cleaner and sleepier than Manila. On my first night I sit on the promenade and watch the light fade over the South China Sea.

Islam is the official religion. All the girls and women wear headdresses of different colours. A few men wear the Islamic headdress of *songkok*, an oval rimless hat, but it's less common. I lunch at a food court where the system is to order, sit down and hold off on paying until they bring the food. The two girls who take my order keep peeping at me, and giggle and blush whenever I look their way. My first bite in Malaysia is of *murtabak*, a thick pancake filled with vegetables and drizzled with a sweet chilli sauce. Beside it a plastic bag holds pickled onion and carrot. With a glass of fresh sugar cane juice, the meal totals to less than a US dollar.

I spend the afternoon browsing around KK, discovering a bookstore with a motley crew of dusty titles left by backpackers over the aeons, and after checking into a downtown hostel venture forth for an early dinner. At a Muslim restaurant nearby the cook stir-fries my order of noodles together with soy sauce, egg, chilli and strips of cabbage blackened from the char of the wok. A glass of *teh tarik* - "pulled tea"

- is sweet milk tea poured back and forth, back and forth between containers until the aerated top froths up like a cappuccino. After lunch this meal is a blowout, equivalent to two whole dollars.

Back in my room I lie on the bed with the soundtrack of noises from the street outside. When I get up in the middle of the night to go out to the bathroom, something large and black scuttles quickly away into the shadows.

· · · · · · · · · ·

In Borneo's south is the province of Sarawak and its capital Kuching, "Cat City". Giant feline statues are everywhere, and a museum even exists dedicated to cats. Another museum was originally the home of James Brooke, an Englishman who assumed control of the land around modern-day Sarawak in 1841. The "White Rajah" and his descendants governed for another century, until after the Second World War.

I hit the ground and walk, getting deliberately lost and letting the place reveal itself. A particular reward is meeting the people - lots of hellos, shy smiles, kids wanting to play peekaboo, impromptu English lessons. It is Ramadan in Malaysia and for a month observant Muslims cannot eat, drink, smoke or have sex during daylight hours. Everywhere are advertisements for the Ramadan buffets come nightfall as the starving citizens slake their appetites.

The Cultural Village near Kuching is where you go when you're not prepared to spend a few days travelling out to stay at a real longhouse with one of the tribes. Sarawak is a major producer of pepper. A lady at the village demonstrates how the green berries of the pepper vine are picked unripe and dried in the sun to become black peppercorns, or soaked in water and the skins rubbed off for the white variety.

It feels fitting then to eat plenty of pepper while in Kuching, in honour of the local spice. First up is the local version of peppered steak at the Telag Usan coffee shop, run by members of the Orang Ulu tribe. A restaurant a short walk from there sells black pepper chicken rice, while a nameless stand opening up outside a convenience store specialises in "black pepper burger" as well as a "chicken gravy hot dog". I'm the stand's first customer of the day, but in the end the most exciting thing about their two products is the names.

The store opposite the stand sells ice cream flavours of avocado, corn and black glutinous rice. Thirsty? Pepsi "Gold" is pee yellow instead of the usual brown.

At breakfast the next day four fat prawns sit atop a bowl of noodles, shredded chicken, bean sprouts and coriander leaves in a spicy, brick-red coconut soup. This is *laksa*, Sarawak style, as served at Chong Choon who are famous for their version, the colour darker than *laksas* in other regions.

The *laksa* turns out to be the best meal of the day. I want to find a local dish called *umai* that sounds like the Latin American *ceviche* - raw fish combined with lime and chilli, with acid from the citrus "cooking" the fish – but am not having any success. I settle for a bowl of another Kuching favourite, tomato *mee,* but it's difficult to be too excited at what, in this rendition at least, tastes like instant noodles in watered-down ketchup. I do appreciate my beverage - a young coconut, its top hacked off and a straw and spoon inserted for sucking up the clear juice and digging into the soft, white flesh.

At the front of another store selling noodle soup a woman is monitoring a giant cauldron of roiling broth, indeterminate animal parts floating in it which she regularly scoops out while adding fresh material in. This broth forms the base of the soup, and as each order comes through fresh noodles are dunked in it quickly to heat them through.

All the seats are taken by customers, and they give me a plastic bag of soup to take away. I make a tabletop out of the only horizontal surface nearby, the lid of a garbage can. I spoon noodles into my mouth with chopsticks while wondering just how porous the bag is, and if this is true hygienic folly. Just how dumb am I being? But my luck holds this time around, and there are no consequences.

. . . .

Semengoh Wildlife Reserve outside Kuching rehabilitates orang-utangs which have been injured, orphaned or born into captivity, with the goal of releasing some back into the wild. In early morning the rangers go to feed the animals, allowing the few tourists who have turned up a possible sighting. A trail out into the forest leads to a covered lookout onto a small wooden platform, where the ranger places some bananas and coconuts and calls out several times.

There is silence except for the drip of the rain and bird and insect noises. Then crashes come in the distance - shadowy figures glimpsed moving in the mist through the shroud of treetops. A female orang-utang emerges with baby on back and an older child in tow. Gradually they make their way to the platform, swinging from tree to vine, and as we watch scoop up a couple of bananas and the coconut, which the mother breaks apart on the side of a tree. It takes her a few tries. Not that I would have done any better, I was lucky – in Kuching mine had been opened for me.

. . . .

Singapore: metropolis of huge malls, frenzied shoppers, spotless sidewalks and beautifully flushing bathrooms that bring a tear of joy to the backpacker's eye. A city which is usually considered clean to the point of antiseptic is currently choked in haze by smoke drifting across from Indonesian forest fires, set by plantation owners and loggers. International relations strain as pollution levels reach unhealthy limits.

The hostel is noisy and the shower cold, but the weather is so humid it's no issue, and it's just across the road from Fort Canning, where a garden grows over a hundred varieties of herbs and spices. Lemongrass stalks can be plucked out of the ground, bruised in water and used as a brush to rub their oily residue across the skin as a natural mosquito repellent.

In a 250-square-mile country with 35,000 licensed food vendors, Singapore can sometimes feel like one huge open-air restaurant. The local diners power their way through Malay, Chinese and Indian dishes, as well as the local *Nonya* cooking that melds those cuisines. It's daunting at first to consider all the options, the thousands and thousands of food stalls in outdoor hawker centres and air-conditioned food courts.

But KF Seetoh, editor of Makansutra eating guide - highest rating "Die Die Must Try" - has persuaded twelve of the best to either relocate or clone themselves in a strip of park facing the marina. This is Glutton's Bay. At twilight the crowd moves from stall to stall, nibbling on chicken wings that have marinated for ten hours before reaching the grill, skewers of mutton, beef and chicken *satay* and *roti kaya* - buttered toast fingers dipped in an eggy coconut custard.

Another way to prioritise which hawkers to visit in Singapore is choose those who've stood the test of time - with some sense of urgency too as their owners age or retire. The proprietor of Ah Kow has been dishing up his tasty mushroom minced pork noodle soup for over half a century. Several other stands have also clocked up nearly fifty years of business. Maxwell Road stall number ten's "Chicken Rice" (a contender for national dish, more on that below) is a relative newcomer, open for just four decades.

Lining up for lunch is a not uncommon pastime. Each food court seems to always have a long queue outside a few of their holes-in-the-wall. One midday, the line of people waiting for Inspirasi food stall to open stretches across the busy food court and out onto the other side of the street. That's OK, as I am the first in the line.

Out in suburbia an establishment named Eng Seng has Singaporeans waiting in line for an hour if necessary for the house speciality, crab. Singapore chilli crab is best known overseas, but here at Eng Seng a black pepper version gets equal or higher billing. I've never tried to eat a whole crab before and don't do a very good job - lots of waste, but the peppery sauce is the main thing. It would go very nicely with prawns or other shellfish too, just about anything really (ice cream may be pushing it). It seems especially suited to the marine sweetness of the crab.

. . . .

The bus from Singapore up into peninsular Malaysia stops only to clear customs and for a bathroom break, as the coach has no facilities. The forest surroundings give way to shack shanty towns, and then wobbly-looking apartment buildings and skyscrapers and we are in downtown Kuala Lumpur. At first glance KL is less friendly than Borneo Malaysia had been, and more overtly religious and patriotic. Flags fly everywhere and Islamic dress for both sexes is more prevalent, although teenagers are teenagers as everywhere and can be seen in miniskirts or weird haircuts designed for maximum provocation.

After hyper-clean Singapore, where you could probably eat off the sidewalk if so inclined, this is a transition again to a big, crowded, dirty city, although KL boasts some impressive architecture which includes the Petronas twin towers, the world's second tallest building (a local insists to me that it's world's tallest). Aesthetics aside, this city has the largest representation of peoples from around Malaysia, meaning for a gastronaut that the cuisines of Penang and Jakarta and the Klang Valley are all to be found here.

I check into an Indian-run guesthouse, the cheapest accommodation of the trip so far, even after upgrading from a dormitory to a "single room" with a thin partition dividing it from the others. I used to be able to sleep through anything, but those days seem to have gone - loud conversations all night and the sounds of various bodily functions through the thin walls mean a sleepless night until an exhausted dawn. My legs are spotted with red bites - fleas or bedbugs? – an unwilling donation of blood to the local insects.

I'm sure I should be out and about in KL rather than spending any time in its air-conditioned malls. The locals, however, are seeking respite in them, and my guilt is assuaged enough to join them rather than suffer in the heat for authenticity's sake. Inside the mall is a shop sign: "Foot Massage/Reflexology". I have been walking a lot. A cute girl waves me in. No sooner have I entered than she delivers me over to a wizened character who pounces on my aching feet and proceeds to find every tender point in the soles and calves and torture them mercilessly. After half an hour of gritted teeth I escape, and hobble back out into the street.

· · · · · · · · · ·

Chowing down with the locals at one restaurant and food stall after another, often far from the tourist trail, I'm a frequent centre of attention and often glance up mid mouthful to find people frankly staring. They are giving The Look, which is saying "What are *you* doing here?" Their stares aren't rude, just bewildered.

It's the sort of attention I get when, on a dust street lined up and down with food stalls, in the shadow of two dilapidated apartment blocks, I stop at Antarabangsa. I wave away the flies that are buzzing about and settling on my upcoming meal, and make my selections. *Nasi lemak* is a plate of rice flavoured with coconut oil and topped with a choice of assorted dishes. First choice, *rendang*, is large chunks of beef coated in spice and cooked in coconut milk until the liquid has evaporated and the meat browns darkly in the rendered fat. The server selects a piece and snips it up into bite-size pieces with scissors. A piece of crunchy fried chicken and a dollop of the chilli sauce *sambal* complete the plate.

Chinese restaurant Siew Ngap Fai expertly roasts goose the Cantonese way so the fat melts away to leave tender, juicy meat and burnished skin - a few slices are draped across a mound of rice with sauces of sweet plum and garlicky chilli. (Goose, to the uninitiated, is like a beefier, darker-meat duck.)

The mission for dinner is to find and consume a Ramly burger. They're said to appear just after nightfall outside or near 7-Eleven convenience stores. Street after street offers no success, although lots of other tempting, and not so tempting, treats. Then - at last! - a man has set up a stand and is cooking up the hamburgers, wrapping them in wax paper to go for each customer.

The Ramly burger is shallow-fried on a griddle with vegetables and condiments (sweet chilli, mayonnaise) placed on top of the patty - so far nothing unusual. But then a beaten egg is poured onto the sizzling fat on the griddle to make a thin omelette, the burger with its toppings folded up in this to create a neat, mess-free package that is slipped between the two halves of the toasted hamburger bun. Greasy, and good.

Ramadan continues, so all the Muslim restaurants are empty and quiet until about seven in the evening and then suddenly packed with ravenous customers. Meanwhile the Chinese places, without any restrictions, do a roaring trade all day long. Lunch at Heng Kee is *bak kut teh*, "ribs tea", a Malay-Chinese soup of pork belly, rib bones and other cuts simmered with Asian vegetables and tofu. Saucers of raw garlic and fresh chilli are at hand to boost the taste up to your liking. By dinnertime I am out of KL proper and in nearby Petaling Jaya at a hawker stand to try *hokkien mee,* a stir-fry of thick yellow noodles and dark soya sauce tossed with shreds of meat, ribbons of cabbage and pork cracklings.

· · · · · · · · · ·

Another bus flees the big city two and a half hours south to Malacca for chicken rice balls. Chicken rice, originally a Chinese dish from the Hainan province, has been adopted with enthusiasm by Malaysia and Singapore. The chicken is poached in water and the resulting broth used to make the rice served with it. In Malacca they take things a step further, removing the chicken from the bone and forming the cooked rice by hand into golf ball-sized dumplings. Sliced cucumber and chilli and soy sauces come on the side.

Two Malaysians, a high school teacher and his lab assistant, have driven down from Sehgor for lunch, and as we tuck into the rice balls at a communal table they discuss the relationship between Malaysian and Indonesian food (Indonesia my next stop) and why the same terms appear on both menus - *rendang, satay, nasi, ayam*.

"The Malay are native people of both Indonesia and Malaysia," explains the teacher. The early afternoon light glints on his spectacles. "But here we have become more multicultural, with a larger Chinese and Indian population."

"So many Malaysian dishes are Chinese or Indian in origin?"

"Yes, but adapted to local tastes. People who came here from China married the Malay and the descendants are called *Nonya*. *Peranakan* are women and men are called *Baba*. So, you have *Nonya* cooking – a mix of traditions. Another rice ball?"

One creation of this tradition is the crumbly tart filled with pineapple jam I snack on after the chicken rice. Malacca was once a Portuguese colony, and that's why restaurants here, like the San Pedro, serve another local tradition - Eurasian cuisine (the product of intermarriage again; this time between Portuguese and the local Malay). "Devil Curry" for dinner turns out to not be as hot as the name implies.

Watching TV at my hotel afterwards, the elegantly-coiffed, expensively-dressed presenter says "I think there's something really beautiful and charming about subsistence".

· · · · · · · · · ·

Padang, Sumatra, gets little tourism these days. I am the only non-Asian to arrive at the small airport, and upon clearing customs waiting taxi drivers descend on me like gulls on an errant crumb. Even after choosing one I am still fending off further offers. Over the next few days I see only a handful of Westerners, all of them staying at the same hotel as me.

The drive into sleepy Padang passes tall palm trees, roadside shacks of wood and weather-beaten corrugated iron, dogs and goats moving in the street. Children brandish toy pistols and shotguns. Motorbikes are the family transport with mum, dad and several kids all wedged together onboard, the horn serving as turning or lane change indicator.

Minang Kabau (Padang) cooking is chilli hot and suffused with spice. As this is a Muslim country no pork is involved, but chicken or goat are used and above all the locals are big beef eaters. A reason to come to this part of Indonesia has been the lure of *rendang*, its best known dish. Originating in Sumatra, it's now popular and widespread all across Indonesia and Malaysia, and these days becoming better known in the wider world beyond.

Large pieces of beef (or, traditionally, water buffalo) are rubbed with a spice-laden paste and then simmered in coconut milk for hours until most of the milk has evaporated and been absorbed into the pieces, now frying in the rendered coconut oil left behind. The meat is supremely flavourful, having drawn in all the spices, and fork-tender due to the long cooking time.

James Oseland, editor of *Saveur* magazine and author of *Cradle of Flavour*, a cookbook on this region, points out that *rendang* is prepared in exactly the reverse manner of a Western stew, in which the meat would be first browned in fat and then simmered in liquid. James has taken the trouble to email me recommendations for the hotel I am staying at, dining tips and several eateries to try. He had warned that everything comes to a standstill during Lebaran, the Muslim holiday following Ramadan, and with impeccable timing that's when I have arrived in Padang and so find several of his suggestions closed - luckily not all.

Here's how a Padang restaurant works: after entering and taking a seat, a glass of warm tea or water and a plate of rice are brought over to you. Then the dishes that were displayed out the front start arriving at your table, until it is covered with small bowls. After you have eaten you are charged only for the bowls you have sampled. With no cutlery supplied, you eat with your right hand (although my limitations with this technique are soon evident and a fork and spoon quickly appear). The presentation of the rice with multiple side dishes reminds me of the *rijstaffel* (rice table) at Indonesian restaurants in the Netherlands, and this makes sense as the Dutch are former colonists of Indonesia.

At Rumah Makan Pagi Sore, recommended by James, nine bowls surround my rice: *rendang*, of course; tough chicken wings; beef jerky fried to crisp shards; stewed cabbage; sliced cucumbers, and three kinds of beans: thin green ones next to white ones combined with *petai* or "stink beans" (not as bad as they sound). Potato cakes look a bit like Dutch *croquettes*. A couple of fish dishes round out the selection: one a curry and the other a whole grilled fish smothered in chilli paste.

Versions of *rendang* outside Sumatra have been a thick stew, the meat teetering on the verge of falling apart and its sauce a rich, oily brown reduction. But in Padang they reach this point and just keep on going - and then some more for good measure. The colour is black and it's now almost dry; the bowl contains a piece of meat, a pool of oil and a grainy sediment that is all that remains of the cooking liquor. Even after such long cooking the meat has still a definite chew - as this one is indeed water buffalo - but is extremely savoury and complex.

Later I leave the hotel for another recommended place. Armed with a map and directions, I set out with quiet confidence, but as usual become hopelessly lost. Although as far as I can tell I'm only a street or two away from my destination, I also seem to be going in circles. A taxi approaches and I flag the driver down and show him the restaurant name.

"Yes!" he says and I get in and off we drive.

We go left, right, left, right, right again, over bridges and through side street after side street. At first it's fun; waving kids excited to see a foreign face, lights twinkling open as Padang settles into twilight. We eventually seem to be leaving the city altogether, and as night falls fewer and fewer houses are on the road sides.

I have realised by now that the driver has no idea where the restaurant is and appears to be just driving around hoping I'll spot my destination. Or is this something more sinister? Am I in the process of being abducted? If so, who will pay the exorbitant ransom my ego will demand I'm worth?

He is ignoring my increasing agitation, until after some insistence I get him to pull over.

"Do you know where we're going?"

"Yes."

"How much longer will it take to get there?"

"Yes."

"You don't, in fact, speak English, and we're completely lost, aren't we?"

"Yes."

Eventually we communicate that he's to take me back to the hotel, and after another long journey we reach it. I give him some money – his one-word English is still better than my Indonesian. Quite a while has passed and still no dinner, and I venture out again, walking this time. In the dark streets I recall a childhood comfort food, my aunt's *nasi goreng* or Indonesian fried rice. This is what I order at a beachfront stand where you can no longer see the Indian Ocean, only hear its waves smacking ashore. It's a tasty enough version, but my stomach percolates for the rest of the night.

· · · · · · · · · · ·

James Oseland had suggested getting in touch with his friend Hasan, a Padang local, and I do so in the morning. Although it's Lebaran, when family gather together and a stranger is almost certainly imposing, Hasan and his family could not be more hospitable. With no advance notice - unaware of my existence until a moment ago - he comes to pick me up and takes me for a tour about town, before heading to his house to introduce me to his wife and daughters. We sit in the shade chatting, drinking Cokes and snacking on mango cheeks.

For lunch Hasan picks a busy spot near the main market. Once again the bowls start accruing on the table; this time stewed liver and deep-fried lung new inclusions. Two other dishes that stand out are *dendang balado*, flat sheets of dried beef coated with chilli and *ayam bumbu*, fried chicken in a breading of coconut, garlic and spices.

Having tried several plates of *rendang* by now the end results can be quite different, and I decide that in one place it is just plain burnt. After working on a big pot-full for so many hours, even the most conscientious cook might not want to start over.

Satay is a word I have always associated with a peanut-based sauce, but it turns out that this is true for only certain parts of Indonesia. *Sate Padang* are grilled skewers of beef, not with a peanut dip but a broth made from offal and thickened with rice flour, which resembles nothing so much as the gravy that would be served with a roast in the UK. European influence again, or coincidence?

NASI GORENG (INDONESIAN FRIED RICE)

Adapted from two recipes: one from my aunt Anne, given to her by a Dutch friend who had been in Indonesia during the Second World War, the other from a Singaporean restaurateur.

This is best started a day before serving or at least in the morning. After steaming the rice it needs to cool and dry so it doesn't become mushy when stir-fried.

Lap cheong Chinese sausages are available vacuum-packed at Asian supermarkets. If not available, substitute 5 rashers (slices) of streaky bacon.

Serves 4. Prepare ahead: Cook the rice 6-24 hours ahead and refrigerate. Approximate cooking time: 30 minutes

2 cups long grain or jasmine rice

3 dried Chinese sausages (lap cheong),
about 150 g (5 ounces) total

Pinch of salt

2 tablespoons vegetable oil, divided

1 large waxy potato, boiled, cooled, peeled and cut into small dice

3 brown shallots or 1 medium brown onion, very finely chopped

450 g (1 pound) minced (ground) beef, 10-15% fat

2 medium tomatoes, finely chopped

2 tablespoons Maggi Seasoning or mushroom soy sauce,
divided, plus extra as needed

2 tablespoons sambal oelek (Indonesian chilli sauce),
divided, plus extra as needed

1 cup frozen green peas

4 eggs

1 cucumber, peeled, de-seeded, halved and sliced thinly crosswise.

Put the rice into a medium, heavy-bottomed pot with a tight-fitting lid, place the sausages on top and add 3 cups water and a pinch of salt. Bring to the boil over high heat, reduce heat to lowest setting and gently simmer, covered, until the water is completely absorbed and the rice is tender, about 15 minutes. Lift the lid to make sure the rice is fully cooked and the water is absorbed — if not recover and cook a few minutes more. Remove the *lap cheong* and spread rice in a thin layer onto a baking sheet to cool and dry, then refrigerate for 6-24 hours. Refrigerate the *lap cheong* separately, and slice thinly crosswise before using.

Toss cold rice gently with hands to separate grains as much as possible. Heat a tablespoon of oil in a wok, large deep skillet or frying pan over medium heat and brown the diced potato. Remove to a plate lined with paper towel and reserve. In the same oil, cook the shallots until soft. Raise the heat to high, add the sausage and cook for 2 minutes. Add the beef, the tomato and a tablespoon each of the Maggi and *sambal oelek* and cook, breaking up the meat with a wooden spoon, until it is brown and crisp.

Fold in the rice, peas and potato and the remaining tablespoon each of Maggi and *sambal* and cook until rice is hot with crunchy bits, turning constantly and gently. Taste and season with additional Maggi and *sambal*, if you like. I usually add a bit more of each at this point.

Meanwhile, fry the eggs in the remaining tablespoon of oil in a separate pan sunny side up (if working solo, you can do this just beforehand and keep warm in a low oven).

Serve the *nasi goreng* immediately with a fried egg atop each portion and cucumber on the side, with additional *sambal* and Maggi on the table for diners to add to taste.

RENDANG (DRY BEEF CURRY)

Rendang is originally from Indonesia, but this recipe is based more on the versions I ate in Malaysia, where they are not cooked for as long and have more sauce. It's best cooked a day before, refrigerated overnight and reheated, as the flavours are more harmonious then. Serve warm with steamed rice.

Serves 4-6. Prepare ahead: Cook the rendang a day ahead. Approximate cooking time: 4 hours.

1 kg (2.2 pounds) beef cheeks, cut into approximately 7½ cm (3 inch) pieces

2½ teaspoons salt, divided, plus additional as needed

2 tablespoons vegetable oil, plus additional as needed

6 tablespoons unsweetened desiccated coconut

5 small garlic cloves, sliced

8 brown shallots, roughly sliced

4 medium fresh red chillies, cut in half lengthways
(de-seed if desired to reduce heat)

1 large knob of ginger, peeled and roughly sliced

2 400 ml (14 ounce) cans of unsweetened coconut milk, chilled

1 lemongrass stalk, peeled and lightly crushed

2-3 kaffir lime leaves (optional)

A few curry leaves or 1 bay leaf

1 cinnamon stick (optional)

Sugar

1 lime

One day ahead: Preheat oven to 150 C (300 F). Pat beef dry with paper towels and season all over with 1 teaspoon of the salt.

Heat the oil in a Dutch oven or large heavy-bottomed ovenproof pan over medium-high heat and sear the beef well on all sides, working in batches to avoid crowding the pan. Add extra oil if needed. Remove beef to a plate and wipe out the pan.

In a smaller frying pan, toast the coconut to a light brown over low heat, stirring occasionally. Cool. Put it into a blender or food processor along with the garlic, shallots, chillies, ginger and remaining salt. Open one of the cans of coconut milk, remove and reserve the solid white cap of coconut cream, and add ½ cup of the clearer coconut milk liquid into the blender. Blend well to make a paste.

In the pot in which you browned the beef, heat the reserved coconut cream over medium heat. Add the paste and fry until it is fragrant and smells cooked rather than raw, has darkened, and the oil has begun to separate out around the sides. Add the beef and any juices that have run out of it and stir.

Add the lemongrass, kaffir lime leaves, curry leaves or bay and the cinnamon stick, if using. Add the rest of the coconut milk from the first can. Remove the hard coconut cream from the second can and discard or reserve for another use. Add the remaining milk to the pan. Bring everything to a boil over high heat, stir, cover with a tight fitting lid and place in the preheated oven for 2½ hours.

Remove the pot from the oven and place on the stovetop. Simmer uncovered over medium heat until the beef is fork-tender, and the sauce is dark and thick and coats the meat. Stir often and watch and smell carefully to make sure it is not burning, lowering the heat if necessary. Now taste the sauce and adjust the seasoning with more salt, sugar and freshly squeezed lime juice to taste.

Chill overnight. Fat will solidify on the top of the sauce, and you can remove and discard some of it if you like. Reheat the *rendang* and adjust the seasoning again. Remove and discard the lemongrass, cinnamon stick and lime and curry leaves. Serve warm.

BLACK PEPPER PRAWNS

Prawns are used here as a substitute for the crab I had in Singapore. Eat with your fingers and plenty of paper towels or napkins, dunking the prawns in the sauce.

Serves 2 as a snacking dish.
Approximate cooking time: 5 minutes

300 g (10 ounces) peeled and deveined king
• or tiger prawns (jumbo shrimp), tail-on

2 tablespoons oyster sauce

2 teaspoons dark soy sauce

1 tablespoon cognac or other brandy

1½ teaspoons freshly ground black pepper

2 tablespoons butter

2 small garlic cloves, finely sliced

2 thin slices fresh ginger,
peeled and cut into fine matchsticks

½ fresh small red chilli, finely sliced (optional)

If the prawns have not already been deveined, make an incision with a sharp knife along the back of each and remove and discard the black thread-like intestinal tract.

Mix the oyster sauce, soy sauce and brandy together in a small bowl. Toast the pepper in a medium heavy-bottomed skillet over medium heat for 1 minute or so until it smells aromatic. Transfer to a small bowl and wipe out the skillet.

Put the skillet back over medium-high heat. Add the butter, garlic and ginger and chilli (if using) and stir-fry for about 30 seconds until they smell aromatic. Add the prawns and stir-fry just until they start to turn pink, about 30 seconds.

Sprinkle the ground pepper over the prawns, then add the sauce and cook quickly until it reduces and coats the prawns. (If some of the sauce caramelizes on the bottom of the pan, add a tablespoon or two of water and stir and scrape to loosen and dissolve it back into the sauce.) Serve.

Variation: Use 450 g (1 pound) shell-on and head-on prawns, and double the rest of the ingredients. You will end up with about the same amount of prawn meat as the above recipe, and it will be a messier job for each diner to peel their own, but the heads and shells will add extra savour to the sauce.

HONG KONG, MACAU, MAINLAND CHINA & TIBET

....,..................

Yung Kee on Hong Kong Island has been famed for decades for its roasted goose, doled out in multiple courses like duck in the Peking manner. Showing up as soon they open, and making my way past a curtain of dark goose-liver sausages to the upstairs restaurant, I place my order for the goose. There is a problem.

"The goose, you see, is for eight people," says the waiter.

After some polite insistence the courses start to arrive, begun by a Thousand Year Old Egg – in reality preserved for several weeks at most - with its greenish yolk and outer white turned translucent black. Thin flour pancakes with wisps of the lacquered goose skin follow, and then a platter of the stir-fried flesh. Assembled waitstaff accumulate and stand around watching me tackle the dishes. One whispers furtively into a walkie talkie.

Hong Kong is all about real estate. So many people and so little space and the only way to go is up, so it is packed with very tall, very thin apartment buildings, their windows strung with laundry. On Kowloon side the busy streets are lined with shop after shop all selling the same things: medicinal foodstuffs, giant shark fins, assorted mushrooms. Sidewalk trays of dried seafood and Chinese sausage marinate in the fumes from the passing traffic.

It's also expensive, especially coming straight from the cheaper parts of Asia. Belatedly, I recall my brother making a trip here while teaching English in mainland China and being broken by the cost of his first beer. I head to the YMCA to check in, but a mix-up means they have neither a reserved room for me nor a vacancy. After some fruitless searching - both a public holiday and a trade fair are on and the town is full – I'm eventually settled into a modest hotel, paying a nightly rate that could fund a small country for several weeks.

The Hong Kong island side is slightly less congested than Kowloon and more interesting. In the markets of narrow laneways recently-live fish still wriggle in their trays. Antique stores carry carvings of a surprisingly raunchy Buddha – he's cross-legged but not alone, if you know what I mean. The wooden-seated Star Ferries have been crossing Victoria Harbour day and night since the late 1800s, and the fare is still a pittance for one of the world's most scenic rides. On the island side near the terminal women squat on pieces of cardboard, sharing snacks and bottles of tea.

. . . .

It is much cooler here, more pleasant to walk in than the swelter of South-East Asia. In the grey mornings *tai chi* practitioners fill the parks and open areas. Their graceful slow motion makes them appear to be moving through a different dimension. An ancient in flowing white pyjamas conducts a session, equipped with modern headset mike and boom box blaring out strident music.

Holes-in-the-wall are full of locals but can be disappointing: bowls of greasy noodle soup heavy with monosodium glutamate, topped at times with a few chewy slices of gristled meat, and in one place a long black hair for textural interest. But Chung Kee in Sheung Wan has a bowl of soup loaded with delicate wonton-wrapped shrimp, the broth clean and clear. The chutney pork noodles at Mak's have the texture of great handmade Italian pasta. Simple plates of stir-fried greens everywhere are just delicious. Lung King Heen inside the Four Seasons hotel is Cantonese fine dining, serving its dishes in Western sequence. Their soup of roasted goose and tofu, blended with cornstarch into viscosity, is the distilled essence of the bird.

"Chinese food" is not a single entity any more than "European food" would be. The Chinese dishes best known in the West are Cantonese in origin, but that's only one of the main cuisines, which include Sichuan, spicy with chillies and peppers, Mandarin's brittle-skinned Peking ducks and dumplings and noodles favoured over rice and Shanghaiese "red cooked" dishes braised in soy and rock sugar. Hong Kong offers all of these, as well as the lesser-known regional cooking of Chiu Chow, Hunan and more.

In the Times Square building, Water Margin is designed to look like a traditional eating house. Servers in black robes bring boiled peanuts to nibble on, then a *dim sum* lunch including slivers of duck breast wrapped in slim sheets of transparent mung bean – see-through ravioli. Steamed dumplings stuffed with chopped mushrooms and greens are on the bland side, but come alive when blasted from the saucers of chilli oil, black vinegar and soy.

At Chiu Chow Garden in Central (Chiu Chow cooking is a relative of Cantonese), the mashed vegetable soup is decorated with a *yin yang* swirl of pureed spinach. The tastiness of the cold soya goose almost balances the rudeness of the staff. Two hours later I am gazing into bamboo baskets of steamed dumplings at an outlet of local chain Crystal Jade, amused girls at tables on either side instructing me on proper dumpling eating etiquette. Compared to the Beijing style in one basket the Shanghai kind, sauced with black vinegar and julienned strands of ginger, are juicier - a trick achieved by folding a dice of jelly made from pig skin into the minced pork filling. Upon steaming, this congealed stock melts into a soup within the dumpling that flows out when it is bitten into (or accidentally stabbed with a chopstick, if one is as clumsy a dumpling eater as I).

A recent trend is French master chefs making their debuts here. Pierre Gagnaire opened 'Pierre at the Mandarin Oriental' only days ago and it's fully booked for weeks to come, but with luck my call for a lunchtime table coincides with a last-minute cancellation. Known for novel, sometimes wacky dishes and combinations of ingredients,

Gagnaire went bankrupt in the South of France when his creations were too *outré* for the locals. He has since re-launched in Paris, and now here in Hong Kong.

On the twenty-fifth floor of the hotel, a corridor dimly lit with candles ends at a dark-chocolate room where large picture windows look out across the harbour to Kowloon. The meal is memorable without being too bizarre: a single quail's egg yolk, crumbed and fried, deep yellow creamed corn soup blanketed with popcorn and finely chopped egg white, and a dessert of lemon as many textures: jelly, cream, meringue, curd, sorbet and liqueur.

Michelin-starred Alain Ducasse's 'Spoon at the Intercontinental Hotel' is a more conventional meal: macaroni *gratin* and tender lamb fillet with "navarin" jus. *Navarin* is a traditional French mutton and turnip stew. The contemporary touch here is to elevate the protein to a starring role and a leaner and younger cut, with the turnips as a garnish on the plate and the sauce now a light "juice" poured around all.

. . . .

In the former Portuguese colony Macau, an hour or so from Hong Kong by ferry, are the world's best egg tarts. I completely misjudge the distance from the ferry terminal to Lord Stow's Bakery, and do an awful lot of walking until finally flagging a rare passing cab, but this ensures I turn up with an appetite. Fresh from the oven, the tarts are dusted with sugar and glazed like a *crème brulée* - the teeth crackle through this thin skin into the warm custard beneath. The (recently) late owner, Andrew Stow, combined the best ideas from Portuguese, Chinese and his native British tarts to create this ultimate version. He leaves us all a sweet legacy.

When foreign seasonings meet local produce you get the sort of Macanese cuisine Café Litoral specialises in. Here are the hams and roasted *chouriço* sausage of Portugal, its *bacalau* fritters of salt cod and *caldo verde*, potato and kale soup. Other dishes are more unique fusions of Europe and Asia. *Minchi* will seem a bit familiar to anyone who's ever stared down into a plate of hash in a Connecticut diner, or a bowlful of *picadillo* in the Cuban dives of Miami. Minced meat is sautéed crisp with both soy and Worcestershire and served over rice, the starch enhanced with tiny cubes of potato and the wetness of a sunny-side-up egg providing the sauce. The spices of "African Chicken" are tamed by coconut milk, while "Portuguese" chicken is turmeric yellow

· · · · · · · · · ·

"Take Care of Slippery" warns the sign in the bathroom of the guest house.

It takes a while to get used to the national pastime in China of spitting. Better out than in is the principle. Each morning in the big cities starts with a cacophony of sounds, as if half the populace outside are desperately hawking up the contents of their lungs. In restaurants and teahouses the occupants of neighbouring tables will lean across and noisily expectorate on the floor next to you. Out on the street a well-dressed businessman strolls by with a placid gaze, pausing only to place a finger delicately against the side of one nostril and eject a stream of something into the street. These are not the only emissions for the wary traveller to dodge - babies have the backs cut out of their pants, ready for a call of nature anywhere at a moment's notice. Better out than in.

In Chengdu, in Sichuan province in Western China, I pass an idle few hours sipping tea with my friend Li Juan, aka JJ. She has travelled over fifty hours by train to meet me here from her home in the country's south. We are in a bustling teahouse overlooking the lake in the People's Park. Fortune tellers wander table to table, followed by peddlers offering an ear-cleaning service with large metal tweezers.

The varieties of options of tea are as exhaustive as wine or cheese might be in Europe and depend on personal taste and desired effect;

beverage as both social libation and medicinal benefit. The tea isn't strained, and as the hot water saturates the leaves and herbs they fall, and dried whole flowers gracefully unfurl until the bottom of each glass comes to resemble the colourful murk at the bottom of a pond.

Later, walking through the park, spaces open to reveal social gatherings immersed in karaoke, opera singing and ballroom dancing. Latin salsa is in full swing as is swordplay, accompanied by music and beating drums. A group of female *tai chi* practitioners wave us in and, although speaking no English, demonstrate the moves and graciously correct my stumbling efforts. Mostly the assorted groups in the park are the middle-aged and elderly. No doubt their kids are busy texting or playing video games down at the mall.

Chengdu has a constant flow of traffic and at rush hour the bikes, motorbikes and an occasional car invade the sidewalks and jostle for space with the pedestrians. We stop for a street snack of small doughnut balls made from pumpkin and bound with a little glutinous rice. Still warm from the fryer, they seem to leap out of the bag into my mouth. A nearby fast food shop is more comprehensive and less squeamish than its Western counterparts would be. It offers every part of the duck but the quack - heads, necks, tongues, webbing.

The large library of the Wenshu temple is lined with saffron-yellow prayer cushions. This is the oldest Buddhist monastery in the area, Tang Dynasty, and the halls resound with chanting and prayer. At another Sichuan tea house, this time inside a large Daoist temple, it's tea as martial art. The kung fu-robed servers twirl their long-spouted teapots about them and fire the liquid into glasses from a distance and at all angles, including from behind their heads.

···········

You don't just order a meal in China. The arrival of the waiters begins an involved process; a long and sometimes intense discussion between them and the diners at table will last several minutes, going back and forth on the merits of specialty dishes and the balance of the meal. Balance is very important. There should be a soup, a vegetable dish, something fried, a little meat. A lot of food ends up wasted - at restaurant tables I've counted over thirty dishes barely touched, and the Chinese do not seem to do doggy bags. Tea will be drunk during the meal as it is throughout the day. Alcohol surfaces in the evening and is likely to be whiskey.

Thais may like to load on the heat, and Indian can be incendiary, but Sichuan cooking is in a class of its own with the liberal use of both fiery red chillies and the tongue-numbing Sichuan pepper (a shrub unrelated to peppercorns), whose mild anesthetic quality leaves the lips tingling. Many dishes are very oily; meats or vegetables are stewed or fried and more oil poured over them before serving.

Menu descriptions in English can be quite beautiful but unenlightening to the foreign visitor as to what they might translate into on the plate.

"JJ, what do you reckon 'Lifelong good partnership?' is?'"

"Um, JJ...'eight drunken immortals'?"

Luckily Li Juan is at hand to help and she takes charge of the ordering everywhere. She has a friend in Chengdu who is a university teacher, and in the early evening we are with the professor and two of her students at a huge restaurant fashioned in the shape of an ocean liner. We're here for the most popular restaurant dish in these parts, the Sichuan hotpot.

On a burner in the table centre is a large pot of angry red broth, the surface littered with dried chillies and tiny Sichuan peppers (set in the middle of it is a smaller bowl of ordinary soup for the not-so-strong of stomach). Into the seething liquid go the assembled trays of ingredients - sliced hot dogs, meatballs of pork and beef, lotus root and other vegetables. Black fungus and more members of the mushroom family follow, then pig brains, strips of cow stomach and squares of congealed duck blood. We fish around in the bubbling mass with chopsticks and cool each mouthful by dipping it first into a bowl of sesame oil mixed with raw garlic and salt. Dog and cat are popular proteins, unless Li Juan and her friends are teasing me, but they aren't in evidence tonight. Batons of eggplant have been stewed with chillies and aromatics, more oil drizzled over the finished dish.

At Chengdu Restaurant *dan dan mian* is spaghetti-like noodles with a sparse meat sauce, and "tiger's skin" is wrinkled dry-fried green peppers. "Sizzling rice" means cakes of rice crisped in hot oil and combined at the table with a cornstarch-thickened sauce - as soon as the liquid hits the rice, here comes the sizzle.

Ma po doufo ("old spotty face grandmother", says Li Juan) is a Sichuan specialty of creamy tofu and nubbins of ground pork cooked together with bean paste and the inevitable chilli and Sichuan pepper. It arrives awash in a crimson oil, and within a few bites I am sweating profusely and reaching for napkins to stem my running nose. Steamed pork spine with pumpkin brings no respite, again laden with - you probably guessed it - pepper and chillies. Some relief for the uninitiated comes from a soup of cucumber and preserved duck egg, and a steamed pudding of pork set into a soupy sauce of tofu and jujubes. Paired with the hot, peppery, oily dishes around it, it seems positively mild and light.

A Buddhist vegetarian restaurant in the grounds of a large temple uses gluten, mushrooms and bean curd to form intricate simulations of meat which in texture and flavour really do resemble the real thing. Here is what looks like duck, with its layers of fat and crunchy skin. The table groans seemingly with whole fish in sweet and sour sauce, sausage, chicken and ham layered with mushroom and bamboo shoots - all of it completely vegetarian. The final dish, at first glance corn with pine kernels, turns out to be - corn with pine kernels.

....

This being China, each carriage in the overnight train to Shanghai has a faucet of boiling water so everyone can make their tea. I had been too late to book the train ahead of time - "Sorry for the incontinence caused", emailed the Chinese booking agent – but have found an empty compartment. In the morning the dining car is full, not of breakfast goers but sleeping passengers who have slipped a few *yuan* to someone in charge because they couldn't afford one of the compartments. We retreat to ours and make a meal out of instant noodle soup. The rehydrated soup in its styrofoam bowl actually tastes of meat and vegetable for once, instead of just chemicals.

After a brief stop in very modern Shanghai it's on to Hangzhou, one of China's loveliest cities. Rainy Hangzhou is famous for its tea, silk and tourist attraction West Lake. And they have amazing dumplings. Why didn't I know about these before? They are basically a cross between a potsticker and a soup dumpling, with a brown, firmly crusted base but filled with savoury liquid, so much so that after I think I've drunk all out of the first one I still manage to burn my lip.

These better-than-soup dumplings – I learn later they are called *sheng jian bao* - come in an assortment of flavours. I like pork-and-prawn best - the pork-and-crab is a bit funky. At the place I discover that sells the dumplings, the chefs begin to look quite alarmed as I return again and again, staring into the window through which they are at work and not so discreetly scribbling notes on their technique.

I have met up in Hangzhou with Shirley, my Chinese-American friend from Los Angeles, and have dragged her along to the dumpling shop to stare with me at the cooks before we go in and sit down.

"That's the head chef, isn't it?" I ask Shirley as a figure emerges from the kitchen and walks by us.

Her eyes narrow. "Were you going to say we all look the same?"

"Not at all," I protest, but on this occasion, at least, I'm having a little trouble.

· · · · · · · · · ·

Back in Shanghai I'm excited to see the Australian chain Donut King has opened its first store in China. They cook their doughnuts to order so they are warm and fresh - a rarity in the modern age. But in the Shanghai store the doughnuts are cold and premade. The very *raison d'être* for Donut King's potential – denied! The machine to make them is inert, but on and ready to go, its red light winking promise. Can I have a fresh one?

"The machine is clean," explains the server.

Of course! Why sully its pristineness with actual use? On my second attempt at a warm doughnut, the next morning, they walk over to the machine, walk past it, retrieve a stale doughnut and microwave it.

In Shanghai's main park hundreds of older men and women are milling about, chatting while holding aloft signs and photos of young people. Missing persons? No-one seems particularly perturbed. Li Juan makes enquiries. "No, they are matchmaking."

We speculate on the conversations. "This is my son. So, he might not look like much. He has a very good job!"

....

The Sichuan Airlines jet flies west for a couple of hours across frozen mountains before touching down at the small airport of Lhasa in Tibet. (The other option had been a new two-day train service linking Tibet with Western China, complete with oxygen masks for the passengers for the elevation.) From the airport it is another hour by battered bus into town, passing by horse-driven carts, trucks, tractors and motorbikes. The aisle of the bus is wedged with luggage, and at each stop people must clamber over it to get out.

Lhasa is one of the highest cities in the world, set on a vast plain surrounded by brown mountains blotched with snow. The 7th century Potala Palace, former home of the exiled Dalai Lama, looks out across the town from a hill. Multi-coloured prayer flags fly from rooftops and buildings. Although it is below freezing, the sky is a brilliant blue and the sunlight blinding, and it is all too easy to get burnt. Leather-skinned, red-cheeked locals in a mix of modern and traditional dress walk around with the lower halves of their faces wrapped to keep warm. What traffic is around is reckless, drivers careering by - on the roads at least, this really is the Wild West.

At twelve thousand feet above sea level, just walking around is an effort for the visitor. In a convenience store packets of cookies and tubes of instant coffee powder are swollen like balloons from the altitude. I climb the stairs at the guesthouse like an eighty-year-old man. When after a shower I try to apply my roll-on deodorant the ball explodes out of the bottle, spraying the contents everywhere. I spend the first couple of days in bed, alternating between deep, short sleeps with vivid dreams and waking with pounding headaches.

In the summer months Tibet gets an influx of visitors; for the rest of the year only the army, some Chinese tourists and a few backpackers contribute to the economy. Shops and hotels are empty and prices slashed, the desperation evident in the street vendors and homeless who latch on to passers-by. Scarlet-robed Buddhist monks carrying prayer wheels beg for money.

In the main square are rural families in from the countryside to stay the night. It's a brutal existence, eking out a living in a land made mostly of rock. Li Juan buys fruit and biscuits to give out to them. I hand a little girl a mandarin orange and she is dubious, afraid - when she realizes it's a gift, her impassive face splits wide into a spontaneous ear-to-ear smile.

Beside the square, the Jokhana Temple draws pilgrims from all over Tibet. Hundreds of them circle the temple day and night, chanting mantras and spinning hand-held prayer wheels. In front of the entrance they throw themselves to the ground, over and over, some with improvised hand and knee pads to cushion the fall.

Tibetan food seems to be all about carb loading against the biting cold. Starch takes the form of dumplings, noodles, potatoes, and the barley mush *tsampa*. Protein is furnished by yak meat and the cheesy butter made out of its milk, blended with salt for a cup of tea Tibetan style. *Momo* are yak-and-coriander filled dumplings that resemble chunky ravioli or Chinese *jao-zi*, served with a tomato relish or chilli dipping sauce. An alternative version is stuffed with vegetables, mainly cabbage and carrot.

Through a doorway blanketed with Tibetan script is a smoky dive filled with locals - all men. According to Li Juan, the women work while the men sit around every day doing what they are doing here: drinking, playing cards and all ordering the same thing, a hollowed-out bread bowl of chewy yak meat braised with onions. Conversation is sparse, as my non-existent Tibetan meets English that is limited to "hello", "bye bye" and "I love you".

. . . .

Back from Tibet, transiting to Tokyo at Hong Kong Airport, I check in nice and early for my morning flight and wait in the terminal, checking email at a computer café and having a leisurely breakfast. Eventually I decide I should wander over to the gate. When I casually glance up at the clock, it is five minutes to the scheduled departure.

As I come running up to the gate there are no longer any passengers or staff and the flight number has been removed from the board. A lone person in uniform awaits. "Mr Frankham?" he enquires drily. I make it on board in time to get the sort of dirty looks from other passengers I usually enjoy giving latecomers myself.

VELVET CHICKEN AND ALMONDS

This recipe, inspired by a restaurant dish and Barbara Tropp and Stephanie Alexander recipes, illustrates the fascinating Chinese technique of "velveting" the chicken. Before stir-frying it is marinated in corn starch and egg white and then briefly poached in hot oil (I use hot water, which is a lot easier in a home kitchen). The process changes the texture of the protein, and the chicken breast is no longer dry as it can sometimes be.

You can vary the vegetables used to whatever you like, bearing in mind that some vegetables need a longer cooking time than others. Harder vegetables like broccoli florets should be blanched in boiling water first for a couple of minutes, to par-cook them before they are finished in the stir-fry.

Serve with steamed white rice or noodles.

Serves 4. Prepare ahead: 'Velvet' the chicken for at least 30 minutes, up to one day ahead. Approximate cooking time: 10 minutes.

2 boneless chicken breast halves,
total weight about 450 g (1 pound)

1 egg white

½ teaspoon salt

1½ tablespoons cornflour (corn starch), divided

½ cup (125 ml) unsalted chicken stock (see appendix)

4 tablespoons light soy sauce

2 tablespoons Shaoxing rice wine or dry sherry

1 teaspoon sugar

3 tablespoons (45 ml) vegetable oil

2/3 cup (100 g) whole blanched almonds

2 brown shallots, very finely sliced

1 tablespoon minced garlic

1 tablespoon minced ginger

2 celery stalks, thinly sliced crosswise

1 medium red capsicum (bell pepper), de-seeded,
cored and cut into thin strips

150 g (5 ounces) snow peas, topped, tailed and strung

1 teaspoon toasted sesame oil (optional)

Cut the chicken into thin, bite-sized strips. Whisk the egg white with the salt and 1 tablespoon of the cornflour in a medium bowl. Add the chicken, mix well and refrigerate for 30 minutes.

Place the remaining cornflour, stock, soy sauce, rice wine and sugar in a small bowl and mix well.

In a wok or large, deep heavy-bottomed skillet bring 4 cups (1 litre) of water to the boil and add 1 tablespoon of oil, then add the chicken meat and stir to separate until the meat is just turning white, 30-45 seconds (the water probably won't return to the boil in that time and that's fine). Drain the chicken in a colander and keep ready near the stove.

Return the wok or skillet to the stove over a medium heat and add another tablespoon of oil. Add the almonds and sauté until browned - remove before they get too brown or they will taste burnt. Drain on a plate lined with paper towel and reserve. Wipe out the pan with paper towels.

Raise the heat to high and add the remaining tablespoon of oil to the pan. Stir-fry the shallots, garlic and ginger just until the shallots are softened, keeping them moving, then add the celery and capsicum and cook for 2 minutes, stirring frequently. Add the snow peas and cook for another 1-2 minutes, until the vegetables are just crisp-tender.

Pour in the sauce and let it quickly reduce and thicken. Stir in the chicken and almonds and cook for about 1 minute until the chicken is cooked through. Sprinkle with the sesame oil, if using, and serve.

Variation: If I have a bottle of it at hand, I like to use 2-3 tablespoons of Stone's Green Ginger Wine in place of the rice wine/sherry and sugar.

JAPAN

Three hours after my plane has touched down at Narita Airport I'm still deep in the depths of the Tokyo rail system, trying to navigate my way to the hotel pre-booked online. At rush hour hired employees stand on the platforms helping to wedge school students and grey-suited *salarymen* into the packed carriages. Eventually I make it to my destination, a modest inn catering mostly to out-of-town Japanese businessmen. The room is tiny and the TV coin operated, but the bathroom is state of the art, a sci-fi compilation of buttons, knobs and flashing lights (alas, with no helpful English signage).

The same futuristic bells and whistles are in the department store bathrooms, with an added bonus of heated seats and dryers that evaporate the moisture from your hands in nanoseconds. Each of the department stores has a food hall in its basement which is a cornucopia of rice crackers and bean-based sweets, assorted teas and street-style snacks of octopus balls and croquettes crumbed in *panko* (Japanese breadcrumbs). In the fruit section, individually-wrapped melons are priced apiece at the cost of a restaurant meal.

When you enter a store or restaurant the staff immediately shout an extended greeting out at you - nor can you slink away without being serenaded out the door. This same sort of greeting occurs whenever passing by any shop assistant or street vendor, almost as if you have tripped an invisible sensor.

Bowing is the essential action I witness, fundamental to Japanese culture. How low and how often to bow seems a matter of both status and occasion. At a railway station a group about to go their separate ways start off bowing to each other and seem unable to stop, each person's response triggering the next round.

Drifting with the crowds of the great metropolis, or alone along quiet backstreets, I see plenty of the local cuisine available but also American fast food chains and their Japanese equivalents, and almost as many *trattorie* and *pâtisseries* as any street in Italy or France.

Restaurants display lifelike plastic models outside of the dishes they serve, a blessing for the visitor who can't read *kanji*. There's a complicated transaction system, however, where you have to purchase a ticket for your selection from a vending machine near the front of the store - which doesn't have the helpful pictures - and only on presentation of that to the staff is the plate prepared.

Shop signs in English read:

"So every oven has the dreams for the breads" (a bakery)

"Tooth Loved" (a dentist)

"Brain Mansion" (...?)

A menu lists its offerings, helpfully translated. Tuna yes, salmon, no worries - but "Young of Punctatus" suggests a 1950s horror movie ("Up from the Depths of Unknown Waters - Comes a Creature to Confound Science!") more than lunch.

In Harajuku fashion district, teenage girls dress to shock - Goth-inspired, safety-pinned punk, short shorts or skirts with knee-high boots. Older women shuffle by them in traditional *kimono*. A man walks three dachshunds, each wearing neck kerchiefs and sunglasses.

··········

For a first taste of sushi, I'm up at 4 am to head to Tsukiji, the world's largest fish market. Every day thousands of tonnes of hundreds of varieties of sea foods are on sale. By 5 am the main action is already over, and both market employees and visitors are forming a line outside Daiwa Sushi, located right inside the market.

Stumbling around in the cold dark I have run into Susan, visiting on business from Washington DC, and Yoko, a local girl who has spent time in the US. A few minutes after Daiwa opens we are crammed into stools around the tiny sushi counter. The three bandanna-ed cooks are already at work slicing and dicing and the head chef is hand-moulding raw seafood onto small slabs of vinegared rice and placing them in front of us. Yoko translates the arrivals - cold and creamy sea urchin, mackerel, shrimp and squid. The fresh fish sparkles in the mouth, underscored by the sting of *wasabi* (Japanese horseradish).

Squares of omelette signal the first round is over, and we can bow out now if we want. Fuelled by the buzz of all that protein, the vast open-air market still remains for us to explore as dawn breaks open. We goggle at huge carcasses of frozen tuna and swordfish, trays topped with octopus tentacles and buckets of writhing eels, all the while in constant danger of being mowed down by the forklifts and trolleys whizzing about.

....

Further sushi adventures begin with Jiro Sushi, to some the best sushi restaurant in the world, refusing to accept my reservation request. No foreigner is permitted at Jiro unless accompanied by a Japanese diner - even another Japanese-speaking foreigner will not do. Kyubei, established in 1936 in the Ginza district, is more accommodating. It's shoes off at the door and then into a small elevator that rises to a room fashioned traditionally with tatami mats and shoji screens. Other diners, Japanese and a couple of Americans, are already seated cross-legged or kneeling around the sushi counter and the fish on display there, whittled into blocks of red and pale pink.

Here is the art of sushi practised at the highest level -- apprentice sushi chefs can spend years just on mastering how to prepare the rice. There's a real sense of theatre watching the chefs at work carefully cutting their product, forming the rice, brushing their creations with a little soy and squeezing over the merest drop of *sudachi* citrus juice or a minimal grating of the zest.

The raw fish melts in the mouth and the rice beneath is packed tightly enough to hold together in the journey from the fingers to the mouth, but loosely enough that once inside, the tongue can pick up the texture of the individual grains. Flounder is a highlight, and kingfish, and above all *otoro* - fatty tuna belly, meaty and marbled like beef. (Amazing that o*toro* was once considered only fit for cat food and is now so prized.) A few cooked dishes punctuate the sushi bites - broiled eel, savoury egg custard studded with mushroom and water chestnut, miso soup with tiny clams. A piece of seared tuna is dabbed gingerly before serving with minute amounts of raw minced garlic and radish.

Later I do get to go to Jiro Sushi for lunch, with a bemused Japanese friend in tow. The stunningly expensive meal, created by the stern eighty-something owner before us, is certainly an experience, but perhaps one largely over my head. My palate doesn't pick up on such subtleties as the respective fish apparently being kept at different temperatures, or that the octopus has had an hour-long massage before service to tenderize it.

....

Tokyo has much more to offer beyond sushi, and luckily most of it a lot less costly. An avalanche of noodles awaits - fat worms of *udon* in broth, and hair-thin *ramen* (Ippudo is a fine local ramen chain). Spaghetti-like *soba* are Honmura An's claim to fame - as you enter the restaurant to one side is the workshop, where workers are coaxing buckwheat flour into delicate strands. The noodles are cooked, chilled and served with a soy-based dipping sauce plus the still warm, starchy cooking water for its nutrients.

I chase down pretty definitive versions of *tonkatsu* (breaded pork cutlets), pricy Matsuzaka *wagyu* beef (rated higher by some than Kobe), and the resolutely non-spicy Japanese curry with its soothing texture of cafeteria gravy. The unusualness of doughnuts filled with curry or bean pale in comparison with *natto* - sticky fermented soy beans, which are about the least appealing thing I have ever put in my mouth (unaware, as yet, that rotten shark waits patiently for me in Iceland). Evenings find me with excuses to be loitering near the convenience stores that sell frozen snacks of *mochi* - pounded glutinous rice - wrapped around balls of vanilla, green tea or red bean ice cream.

· · · · · · · · · ·

The bullet train hurtles past Mount Fuji to Kyoto, former imperial capital and the city in Japan that has best preserved a sense of life in the samurai era. At Tenruyi, site of Japan's oldest Zen temple (9th century), I walk in the garden added in the 1300s, each side of the path splashed with autumnal reds and golds from the trees. In the historic Gion district the narrow streets are crammed with a flow of visitors who sweep me up in their midst, past tourist trinkets and tearooms, a couple of geisha girls tottering along on their clogs, until I am suddenly deposited in the huge garden of an old temple, completely deserted save for a few croaking crows and a bored security guard.

From there it's a short walk to a place that was advertised in a tourist guidebook for *yakitori* prepared in the local manner. Skewers of chicken parts - breast and thigh, but also heart, liver and gizzards – are smoked with grape branches over charcoal to an underdone state. I prefer my poultry cooked through, but when in Kyoto... "Ovary of Gray Mullet with Salt" on the menu turns out to be fish roe.

Kaiseki, like the French *dégustation*, is a tasting of several small dishes of seasonal ingredients that add up to a full meal. Each part is carefully considered for its contribution to the overall experience. Presentation and appearance are as important as flavour, and the choice of crockery as essential as what's plated on it. At three-hundred-year-old Hyotei I squeeze my legs under the shin-high table in a room of mats and sliding screens. The room overlooks a landscaped garden where carp swim in a tiny pond.

Lunch is a lacquered box divided into four partitions of cold ingredients: bits of fish both raw and cooked; vegetables fresh and pickled, trimmed into neat geometric shapes; a softly boiled egg. The soup and rice are hot, as are a couple of cups of the bitter Japanese green tea. Elegant and aesthetic to be sure, but, to my taste, a meal which is more interesting than enjoyable, of intellectual rather than emotional appeal.

It's another early start across town to the Daitokushi monastery for *zazen*, Zen meditation, in one of the sub temples. From 7 am the students sit cross-legged, every twenty minutes the sound of a clapper allowing a couple of minutes' respite to massage sore and numb limbs back to life. For the latter half of the hour-long session a monk prowls the floor with a large wooden stick, dealing a hefty blow to anyone he feels is not firmly enough in the present moment. Luckily, I am spared the rod.

Afterwards the monk drinks tea and chats with the students - relieved of his weapon he is affable, and speaks decent English.

MAGURO NO TATAKI! (SEARED TUNA)

Raw fish is common in Japanese restaurants. Places like Kyubei restaurant take the idea to the next level, flash-searing the exterior of tuna to create a thin cooked border framing a blood-rare centre. As you're almost eating it raw, buy sashimi/sushi grade fish, the highest quality. A Japanese grocery store may be your best bet to find high-quality fish cut the appropriate way and also the other ingredients.

Serves 2 as an appetiser or side dish. Approximate cooking time: 30 minutes including marinating time

225g (8 ounces) sashimi-grade tuna, preferably in a rectangular block at least 2½ cm (1 inch) thick, free of any sinew and bloodline

2 tablespoons Japanese soy sauce

1½ teaspoons freshly squeezed lemon juice

1½ tablespoons toasted white sesame seeds

1½ tablespoons toasted black sesame seeds

1½ teaspoons coarsely-ground black pepper

3-4 shiso leaves, stems removed

1 tablespoon vegetable or olive oil

1 teaspoon Japanese light sesame oil or olive oil

Place the tuna in a bowl just big enough to hold it. Mix the soy sauce with the lemon juice. Pour over the tuna and marinate it for 30 minutes at room temperature, turning every 10 minutes and occasionally spooning some of the marinade over the top.

Mix the white and black sesame seeds and pepper on a plate. Remove the tuna from the marinade and roll in the sesame seed mixture to completely coat on all sides, pressing them into the flesh.

Stack the shiso leaves together and roll up tightly from left to right to make a bundle, then cut it crosswise into fine ribbons (the French term for this is 'chiffonade').

Heat a heavy-based skillet or frying pan over medium-high heat until a drop of water sizzles and evaporates in seconds. Add the tablespoon of oil and then the tuna and cook for 20 seconds on top and bottom and a couple of seconds on each of the sides (cook a little longer if much thicker than an inch). Remove to a carving board.

Slice the tuna against the grain into 1.25 cm (½ inch) thick slices. Arrange the slices on a serving plate with the rare centres facing up. Drizzle or brush with the sesame oil and sprinkle over the shiso. Eat by picking up the pieces with chopsticks or spearing them with a fork (if you eat them with your fingers, I promise not to tell anyone).

VIETNAM & LAOS

Years ago, working in Cambodia, I had the chance to go to Vietnam at a time when the tourist borders were as yet unopened. It was literally a taxi ride away, but I never made it. Oh well. "Better ever than never", as a European friend used to say.

At Tan Son Nhat Airport I convert my remaining *yen* into *dong* and become an instant millionaire, after Japan's relative calm plunged back into the heat, smells and chaos of South-East Asia. In Pham Ngu Lao, Backpacker Alley, geckos clamber the walls of the winding alleyways. Toddlers and dogs scavenge in the dirt. Ten US dollars purchases a single room in a guesthouse with bathroom, air conditioning and fuzzy satellite TV. Craving something cold and sweet, I buy a Coke - a few sips are enough and I replace the can on my bedside table. In the morning I think about finishing it but decide instead to pour the contents down the sink. The liquid is now full of dead ants.

Ho Chi Minh City, once upon a time Saigon, teems with people, motorbikes with families on board, cars and the tricycle rickshaws called *cyclos*. The blare of horns and the drone of engines go on at all hours. By eight in the morning the back of my shirt is already wet with sweat from the heat as I negotiate with a motorbike rider to take me around for the day.

Deal done, we slip out into the sea of traffic to go inspect the main attractions. First up is the Reunification Palace, where thirty years earlier tanks drove through the gates to signal the end of hostilities in the Vietnam War. The War Museum documents the story of the conflict with first the French and then the Americans.

"You'd think they won it," a twenty-something US backpacker remarks to his friend.

A more serene experience is available at the Jade Pagoda, where you buy turtles at the entrance to release for good luck and then wonder just what happens to them afterwards. A lot of soup is for sale nearby. The interior of the pagoda is a mix of Buddhist and Daoist art and symbolism.

The Cu Chi tunnels are a day trip away and show off a small part of an underground tunnel network that stretched for hundreds of kilometres and was used by the Viet Cong in the war. After a patriotic briefing on the history in rather impenetrable English, some of the hidden entrances to the tunnels are revealed. A gaggle of tourists are invited to descend into inky blackness to crawl through a few hundred metres.

It's just a short passage, specially widened, but with people wedged in front and behind, no light and the air hot and suffocating, it becomes overwhelming to think of someone passing out and trapping us all beneath the earth. I emerge white and shaky, thereby failing to impress Astrid, the Swedish backpacker I had been trying to show off for.

··········

Back in Ho Chi Minh City, the traffic remains incredible. There's an art to master in crossing the roads. Although all instincts scream to make a mad dash for it it's essential to move very slowly, giving the cars and bikes whizzing around plenty of time to see you. Breakfast in this part of the world usually means noodle soup and Pho Hoa, a multi-storey building on Pasteur Street, is full with people sitting around communal tables. Everyone is consuming *pho*, big bowls of beef broth. They arrive containing rice noodles, raw onion and a few slices of brisket, then are loaded up to each person's taste from the other ingredients assembled on the table: plates of blanched bean sprouts, fresh basil and different types of mint, chillies, hot sauce and segments of lime.

Today's hired chauffeur outlives his usefulness when, asked to take me to Quan An Ngon for lunch, he deposits me instead at another destination, insisting it is the right place. No doubt he gets a commission for delivering customers here. Another motorbike whisks me to the right spot. Once settled in at the bar I order *com tam* - "broken rice" - a dish fashioned from the grains damaged during threshing and a Vietnamese comfort food. It is topped with a pork chop, julienned pig skin and a slice of a sort of quiche, infused with the assertive flavour of fish sauce.

Cha gio are next, fat little spring rolls of rice paper wrapped around minced pork, black fungus and carrot and deep-fried to a crusty brown. The diner places a *cha gio* on a lettuce leaf, piles on fresh herbs and vermicelli noodles, rolls up the package and eats, the fresh green tastes playing off against the crunchy grease of the roll.

Light trickles away in the early evening, and an eatery in an alleyway off a main avenue is just some tables with a few electric lights above. It's crowded, while the bigger restaurant across the road remains half empty. The eatery's speciality is *banh xeo*, crisp rice flour crêpes filled with bean sprouts and a couple of chunks of boiled pork, brought sizzling to the table with yet another plate overflowing with various lettuces and herbs. Once again the plan of attack is to wrap up the main attraction with herbs and the lettuces into a parcel and consume, dunking it in either fish or sweet bean sauces.

It is dark now and I am still hungry, and a middle-aged couple sharing the same table help me to order *bi cuon*, "fresh" spring rolls with a bit of protein - here shredded pork meat and skin - rolled up with lettuce, herbs and vermicelli in unfried rice paper. This recurring theme of extravagant use of herbs and leaves brings a lightness to the food in Vietnam, making it less reliant on a lot of meat and fat to draw flavour. (The travellers guides advise you to avoid these fresh salads, so much of what Vietnamese cuisine is about.)

Baguettes and strong coffee are available everywhere in this former French colony, but it is some girls waving me into their hole-in-the-wall the next morning that win out. What looks to again be pho is another noodle soup named *bun moc*, this one afloat with several kinds of processed pork as well as the usual herb garden at hand to add in. It also has meatballs. What's in a meatball in this part of Asia is always something to ponder on, as I remember a menu in Cambodia that proudly proclaimed its balls as made "without sand".

At the other end of the financial dining scale is midday lunch at Lemongrass, a sit-down, glassed-in chairs-and-tables venue aimed at tourists and the Viet expat crowd. Lonely Planet warns it is a "splurge". The splurge amounts to three dollars for three courses: fresh spring rolls, caramel claypot pork and banana cake.

. . . .

Leaving Saigon and heading north to Danang, I hire a taxi and drive south along China Beach to Hoi An, the sky darkening and lightning crackling like veins through the clouds. Hoi An's old quarter with its ancient shop fronts is a taste of colonial days. Blackouts happen each afternoon and evening at the Phuoc An hotel and dogs and cats roam the hallways. The staff however are friendly, the water hot and the air conditioning cold, the price right, and the TV is showing a film with Sean Connery overdubbed by a female Vietnamese voice.

Wandering the dusty streets later, I'm struck by the general lack of interest in privacy. Doors to homes are thrown wide and open directly into people's lives. The passer-by peers into a diorama of Vietnamese going about their business for the evening: eating, grooming, talking and watching TV.

Brother's Café is a marked change from the "restaurants" I've been eating at lately, usually a few plastic chairs on a corner below a hand-lettered sign. A landscaped garden lit with Chinese lanterns leads through to Brother's, set in a colonial-era house facing the waterfront.

A salad of banana flowers is topped with squid, shrimp and sesame seeds and served with rice paper griddled into crisp crackers. Skinless sausages of beef are grilled wrapped in *la lot* leaves. A curry of more beef with carrots is stewed in clear young coconut juice. After all this I don't have room for dessert, but I have some anyway.

Hoi An's central market is a tarpaulin-covered mass of vendors of vegetables and dry goods, various meats and sea creatures. Not far away, along the river by boat, is the Red Bridge Cooking School. White rice, soaked overnight and blended with twice its quantity of water, makes the rice paper that has such a myriad of uses. It's a wrapping for fresh or fried spring rolls, a casing for steamed dumplings, or cut into strips to make noodles.

To make the rice paper, a ladle of batter is smoothed out into a circle onto thin white cotton stretched across a pot of boiling water. To create the *banh xeo* pancakes I had back in Saigon, the same batter is poured into a small frying pan and sprinkled with shrimp. Bean sprouts and chopped green onions go in too, it's folded in half and drained of excess oil before being wrapped up with salad and herbs into rolls. After two attempts I successfully flip my crêpe, splattering hot bean sprouts and droplets of grease onto my Scandinavian neighbour's bare leg.

···········

A rickety bus transports a group of backpackers four hours north. You have to sit carefully, as a fraction too much pressure on the back of your seat sends it plummeting back towards the person behind you. At first the countryside is flat, clumps of ruins, coconut trees in rice paddies, a few buffalo, and farmers who wear the conical hat called *nola*. The bus winds its way up into the mountains, their tops smothered with clouds, past houses of thatch and rusted metal. The road straightens out, and then we are in Hue.

First matter to take care of is *bun bo Hue*, the local spicy noodle soup. I drop my bags at the guesthouse and head to the address recommended by a guide book. At midday it is deserted, a lone waitress chatting on the telephone. The place next door, not recommended, is full of people.

Which to choose? I have a bowl at both. It's similar to *pho*; the soup not as deeply flavoured but with the addition of a couple of white and red sausages in the bowl, packing a nice punch from the cracked peppercorns studded inside the crimson one.

Tu Hieu is a peaceful monastery set among gardens and green ponds. Thich Nhat Hanh, the Buddhist monk and teacher nominated by Martin Luther King for the Nobel Peace prize, was ordained and lived here for a time before being forced into exile in 1966. He made an historic return to the monastery last year. People snore in hammocks, dogs bark at passers-by and young novices in grey smocks go about their duties, thick tufts of hair protruding from bald pates as their heads are shaven in stages. Scattered about are handwritten posters, mostly in Vietnamese but a couple in English:

"Do Not Hurry - Enjoy The Present Moment."

"Breathe And Smile."

I buy a bottle of "Pure Drinking Water" from a vendor in the grounds. On inspection, its origin is "T T Hue Sewerage Company."

Apparently an imperial cuisine of Hue exists, created for the pedantic palates of 19th century royal family. It sounds interesting but turns out to be hard to track down. I do find local favourites *Am Phu* fried rice, a deconstructed version with all the ingredients sorted into neat piles, and *tre,* chopped-up pig enfolded in banana leaf along with a stinging dose of fresh chilli.

··········

Cool, overcast Hanoi is like a different country from lower Vietnam, the strong breeze a refreshing change from the sticky heat of the south. The usual motorbikes and *cyclos* zip around wide tree-lined boulevards, their intersections a tangle of dangling electrical wire. Offices close for lunch for several hours in the middle of the day. Thanks to a power blackout the lobby of my minihotel in the tourist ghetto is candlelit, and I grope my way up the stairs to my room in the dark.

An early bowl of *pho* at Ly Quoc Su in the old quarter is unlike its southern counterpart. In Saigon it was unadorned beef noodle soup, with a plate of herbs and sprouts to the side, but here in Hanoi it comes pre-assembled, with the greens already judiciously added in by the cook. The lunchtime buffet on the ground floor of the Sofitel Metropole presents a grand tour of Viet street foods and desserts of sticky rice sweets.

In the afternoon I take in the water puppets show - an art form over a thousand years old. When I look around me the other tourists are viewing it through the tiny frames of their video cameras and phones for posterity. I seem to be the only one in the audience watching the action unfold for real.

Afterwards on the banks of Huan Kiem Lake I meet Thu, a university student keen to practise her English, and we go for dinner to Highway Four. The language lesson snowballs into half the waiters sitting in, neglecting the other diners. Highway Four's menu gleefully offers locusts, scorpions and stink bugs, crickets and snake wine, but my digestive system feels unable to rise to the challenge this time. We get our insect quota anyway, as a dead fly has been inadvertently grilled in along with the beef rolls.

CHA GIO (MINI SPRING ROLLS)

While rice paper is traditional to wrap these rolls, here I use spring roll wrappers, which seem to absorb less oil. If you can only find large spring roll wrappers, rather than the mini ones called for here, use the large ones. Cut them in four and fill each with about a heaped teaspoon of filling.

An easier alternative to deep-frying is to spray or brush the rolls with oil and bake on a tray at 200 C (400F) for about 20 minutes, turning once, until golden and crisp.

Serves 6-8 (makes about 48 rolls).
Approximate cooking time: 45 minutes.

Hoisin Peanut Sauce:

2 tablespoons smooth (creamy) peanut butter

4 tablespoons hoisin sauce

1 teaspoon freshly squeezed lime juice

Spring Rolls:

1 tablespoon vegetable oil

1 medium yellow onion, finely diced

30 g (1 ounce) dried black fungus, soaked 30 minutes in hot water, removed from water (leaving any sediment in bottom of bowl) and minced (these can also be called cloud ear fungus, wood ear fungus or tree ear mushroom)

1 large or 2 medium carrots, peeled and grated
(about 1 packed cup after grating)

2 tablespoons (30 g) flour

1 large egg, beaten

450 g (1 pound) minced (ground) pork, not too lean

¾ teaspoon salt

½ teaspoon freshly ground black pepper

1 250 g (8.8 ounce) package of frozen small spring roll wrappers, 125mm x 125mm (5 inches square)

Oil for deep frying

To serve:

Romaine or other lettuce sheaves, large enough to
wrap the spring rolls in

Mint leaves and/or Vietnamese basil
and/or coriander leaves (cilantro)

Bean sprouts

Cucumber cut into long, thin strips

To make the Hoisin Peanut Sauce, whisk the peanut butter, *hoisin* and lime juice together in a small bowl. Thin with a few tablespoons of water to a thick dipping sauce consistency.

To make the spring roll filling, heat a small saucepan on medium low heat. Add the oil and onion and cook until slightly softened, about 5 minutes. Add the black fungus and carrot and cook for another minute, then stir in the flour. Transfer to a large bowl and cool.

Add the egg, pork and salt and pepper and combine everything gently but thoroughly until blended. You can poach or microwave a spoonful of the mixture to check the seasoning, and adjust as needed.

Remove wrappers from freezer for a few minutes so they begin to soften and become pliable. Lay 1 mini spring roll wrapper in front of you diagonally and wet the edges by dipping a pastry brush or your finger in a bowl of water. Add 1 tablespoon of filling in the bottom third of the wrapper. Wrap the bottom edge over the filling, tuck in the two side edges, and roll up tightly. Seal the edge with water.

Heat the oil in a large heavy-bottomed pot or electric deep-fryer to between 160 C to 190 C (350 F to 375 F) degrees. If you don't have a thermometer or a deep-fryer, the oil is ready when a pinch of flour floats and sizzles rather than sinking. Deep-fry the spring rolls until golden brown and crisp. Cook in batches, taking care not to overcrowd the wok, which will lower the temperature of the oil and make the rolls greasy. Remove with a slotted spoon and drain on paper towels.

To serve, place a roll inside a lettuce leaf and top with your choice of herbs, bean sprouts and cucumber. Roll up and eat, dunking in the peanut sauce.

Variation: In place of the flour, for a more authentic touch use 60 g (2 ounces) mung bean noodles, which can also be called bean thread, glass or cellophane noodles. Soak them in hot water for 30 minutes and snip with scissors into 5cm (2 inch) pieces.

. . . .

In the outskirts of Luang Prabang in Laos is a Shell service station where the "S" has fallen off, so the big yellow and red sign announces "HELL".

But Luang Prabang is far from hell - on the contrary, to many people it is their heaven on earth. Hardcore backpackers and travellers of my acquaintance have raved to me for years of this, their favourite spot on the planet, their personal Shangri-La, and about the gentle, laid back nature of the locals. Part of its charm may have been that it was not yet on the tourist map. By now it's been very much discovered but LP still has appeal, a picturesque little town of Buddhist *wats* and markets, ringed by the mountains of northern Laos.

I head straight from the small airport to a restaurant for lunch, and when the waiter hears I haven't yet checked into my guesthouse he insists on driving me there afterwards on the back of his motorbike. It turns out to be the wrong, similarly named, place, but it's the thought that counts, right?

Bicycles and motorbikes are the main transport. Monks, their robes saffron here, can be seen everywhere, carrying alms bowls in the morning (they eat twice a day, at five am and midday) and as the day heats up shielding themselves from the sun with umbrellas. An internet cafe is full of the yellow cloth of young monks surfing the web, one texting on his mobile phone. The French influence in this one-time part of Indochina remains in the baguettes on offer in the market and the games of *boules* in progress around the town.

Saturday I slowboat up the Mekong River, terraces lining the banks, to a cave filled with thousands of statues of the Buddha placed there over the centuries. I have thought also about trying to get out to the enigmatic Plain of Jars while in Laos, but it is an eight-hour bus ride from LP and reported to still contain mines and unexploded bombs from the days of the Vietnam War.

....

To describe Lao food as 'Thai meets Vietnamese' is overly simplistic, but it gives some idea. It has Vietnamese-like spring rolls and noodle soups, and every table will have a plate of herbs and raw vegetables. Meanwhile other dishes are identical to those just across the border in Isaan, the north-eastern province of Thailand.

It is the spiciest food I've encountered since Sichuan. The chilli is not cooked into the food to become part of it, but added fresh at the end as a seasoning and prized for its raw and abrasive qualities. My eyes water and my nose runs mercilessly as I cauterise my taste buds. Iced water merely fuels the flames.

Two excellent restaurants in LP are Three Nagas and Tamarind, the latter owned by an Australian woman and her Lao partner. *Nori*-like preserved sheets of river weeds are spread with a thick paste of dried chilli and buffalo skin. Sweet buffalo jerky goes well with pickles of bamboo and green vegetable and dips of fresh coriander leaf, tomato and eggplant.

More familiar for anyone who knows Thai food are green papaya salad and *laap,* called *larb* in Thailand, a warm salad of finely minced raw buffalo or (cooked) poultry with a gritty dressing of herbs, lime juice and toasted rice powder. Native to this region are very good pork sausages, perhaps a descendant of French *charcuterie*, heavy on the lemongrass.

Starch comes in bamboo baskets of white or purple sticky rice. You pick up some with your fingers, knead it together and use it to scoop up bits of the other foods. Lao dishes are quite dry, as this method would be impractical with a lot of sauce. Repeat till replete! Everything is washed down with cups of the smoky local tea.

Nobody here ever seems to need chairs, but rely on the Asian way of squatting on the haunches. It looks easy, but I can report that after only a minute or so, less experienced thighs start to ache.

LAAP (LAO CHICKEN SALAD)

I sometimes substitute soy sauce for fish sauce in this recipe, a heresy and a tip given me years ago by a restaurateur whose menu had to cater to vegetarians. The truth is that fish sauce does not hold the same appeal for me as it does for millions in South East Asia and around the world. In my defence I once fed this *laap* to a Laotian woman in Canada, also a restaurateur. Not knowing I had used soy, she declared it to be better than the versions at the local Thai restaurants.

Increase the amount of chillies if you are a heatseeker (the laap I had in Laos were extremely fiery). Serve with lettuce leaves to use as wraps, or with steamed white rice. Or both!

Serves 4.
Approximate cooking time: 10 minutes

3 tablespoons uncooked rice (traditionally sticky
aka glutinous rice, but use whatever you have)

½ teaspoon sugar

1/8 teaspoon (a pinch) of salt

450 g (1 pound) minced (ground) chicken

225 g (8 ounces) pink/red shallots, halved lengthwise
and very thinly sliced (about 6 small shallots)

Large handful of torn mint leaves

Large handful of fresh coriander (cilantro) leaves

1-4 small fresh hot red chillies, such as bird's eye,
thinly sliced on the diagonal

3-5 tablespoons (45-75 ml) freshly-squeezed lime juice (2 limes)

3-5 tablespoons (45-75 ml) fish sauce or light soy sauce

In a medium saucepan over medium heat, toast the rice until it becomes an even brown colour. Transfer to a spice grinder and blend to a powder (or grind it by hand with a mortar and pestle).

Wipe out the pan and add ½ cup (125 ml) water and the sugar and salt. Bring to a boil over medium high heat. Add the chicken, reduce the heat and simmer for about 3 minutes or until just cooked through. Remove from heat and strain the liquid into a bowl, reserving the chicken in a large serving bowl. Return the liquid to the saucepan and boil until reduced by half. Stir the reduced sauce into the chicken.

Add the shallots, mint, coriander and chillies and mix well. Mix in 3 tablespoons each of the lime juice and fish or soy sauce. Now start tasting and adding more lime juice and fish/soy sauce until you have an even balance of sour and salty. Sprinkle the rice powder over and serve.

INDIA

Visitors to India seem to love or hate the experience, but never leave with a neutral impression or indifference.

"How was it?" I asked my brother, who had just backpacked throughout the country for three months.

"Amazing!" he said. "I'll never do it again!"

It's a nation of extremes that inspires extreme emotions – the worst of poverty, extravagant displays of wealth, modern technology atop age-old traditions. On the flight into Mumbai people change seats constantly – at least four different people in the seat next to mine – and wander about the cabin during take-off and landing while frazzled flight attendants try to keep order. The mild chaos is a taste of things to come.

The City Formerly Known As Bombay, Mumbai is a sprawl of twelve million people facing onto the Arabian Sea. It has the faded charm of weathered buildings and ancient buses (in one case with the passengers out behind the bus, pushing it). Women in brilliantly-coloured saris pass by children playing cricket out front of slum dwellings. Crowds gather along the sea wall and spill onto Chowpatty Beach, where cross-legged vendors ply their trades.

The overwhelming destitution that will be visible everywhere over the next few weeks is already apparent. A girl attaches herself to me and clings on for several blocks until she is gently dislodged with the assistance of a local. A beggar carrying a sleeping baby pinches it sharply to make it cry as I approach.

The Indian caste system has been officially banned but is still in practice, especially in the countryside. Born into a caste, you are traditionally stuck there and for a million lifetimes too – no reinventing yourself this time around through hard work or connections. At the top are the Brahmins, and the system runs all the way down to the Untouchables, who inherit the manual labour and dirty jobs no-one else wants.

Over the centuries reaction against the caste system has produced several religions from within Hinduism, including Buddhism and Jainism. At a Jain temple, chanting devotees ring bells and make offerings of fruit, forming piles of rice into swastika shapes. Strict, strict vegetarians, the Jain won't consume even a vegetable that grows underground, so abstain from onion, garlic, potatoes and carrots. Their mouths and noses are covered with masks, to prevent them accidentally inhaling and swallowing tiny insects.

On nearby Malabar Hill rises the Tower of Silence, actually a well, where the Parsi sect leave their dead above ground to be eaten by vultures. Some birds can be seen floating overhead, but after centuries of this practice they are scarcer now and overfed. The bodies are piling up, and chemicals are resorted to in order to speed up decomposition.

Dobhi wallahs, laundrymen, are at work near the railway station, hundreds of them scrubbing and beating out clothes and linen. Laundry from hostels and hotels across Mumbai ends up here to be cleaned and returned. Meanwhile, the *dabba wallahs* are criss-crossing the city. Each morning they pick up home-cooked meals from wives and mothers and transport them by local rail and foot to the office workers by midday, then collect and return the empty containers in the afternoon. Most of the *dabba wallahs* are illiterate and rely on coloured marks and codes on the *tiffin* containers, an amazingly efficient system dating back over a century. Each business day some two hundred thousand meals are delivered and returned safely. The service costs hardly anything, and they almost never get it wrong.

. . . .

Vivek Bhanushali at Mumbai's Paschim Restaurant does not hesitate when one of the diners expresses concern over the hotness of the prawn curry.

"Yes, it's very spicy. If you have it, you will regret it tomorrow. If you don't have it – you will regret it forever!"

The cooking of the northern Punjab may be what is largely known as "Indian food" overseas, due to immigration from that area to other countries, (for the same reason Cantonese was once synonymous with "Chinese food" and Neapolitan "Italian"). Indian food is so much more, of course – a collection of distinct regional cuisines, reflected in the different combinations of spices and styles.

Generalizing enormously, the divide is of meat, breads and dairy in the north, with cumin as first spice into the pot, while in the south it's vegetables, rice and coconut, and the show kicks off with mustard seeds. The middle of the country around Mumbai has a bit of everything. At a Gurjurati *thali* lunch, servers wander around with pots of vegetables and lentils, which they use to continually replenish the compartmented metal trays (*thalis*) of the diners.

Indian cooking is also food as medicine. A balance based on Ayurvedic principles has developed with many ingredients providing health benefits, and in certain conjunctions reputed to unlock further nutritive values and curative properties. Some forty percent of the world's second most populous country are vegetarian – this is not a culture of a meal built around a large slab of animal protein with accompaniments. Instead, the intricate spicing and the array of vegetables prepared in different ways create very satisfying, meatless repasts. You just don't miss the meat.

. . . .

In Mumbai I link up with a culinary tour, a small group of Americans (and a couple of Australians) travelling about the country. It's led by

Julie Sahni, author of *Classic Indian Cookery* and *Classic Indian Vegetarian and Grain Cooking*. We fly to Goa, the former Portuguese colony, and drive an hour from the airport along the coastline, the van often having to brake or stop for the cattle that wander across the road. By sunset we are at the beach in time for a seafood dinner by candlelight on the sand.

At the next day's tour of the markets the workers in the seafood section aren't keen on being photographed, and if not remunerated properly first are liable to splash the offender from a bucket of fishy water – a smelly souvenir very hard to remove.

Nearly five hundred years of Portuguese presence has left its mark, and in Goa it's easy to find old country staples such as *caldo verde*, *chourico* and *feijoada*, albeit with the spice quotient ramped up. *Vindaloo*, a dish synonymous on international menus with "how hot can you take it?", here doesn't bristle with fiery chillies. Probably starting life as a Portuguese stew of wine and garlic (*vinho de alho*), it has morphed into a coconut-based curry made with pork, a meat rarely consumed in this nation of Hindus and Muslims. The meat is marinated for three days in palm vinegar, garlic, chillies, toasted spices, coconut and *kokum*, a sour tropical fruit. It is cooked slowly, and rested for another day before serving.

Maria de Lourdes Brasto de Costa Rodrigues serves the *vindaloo* and other local favourites such as fish curry and *xacuti* (poppy seed curry) for lunch at her Goa home. Dessert is a cake named *bebinka,* made from a crêpe-like coconut batter baked in multiple layers – Maria's has eight, but there can be as many as twenty. Hours of work are involved, as each layer takes twenty minutes or so to cook through before the top is brushed with *ghee*, clarified butter, the next layer added and the cake returned to the oven. I have *bebinka* from now on wherever I chance across it in Goa – it seems to be spelt various ways but is always delicious. Given the chance, and cooks who don't mind a kitchen project, it could be a meal ender as widespread in popularity as apple pie or chocolate cake.

· · · · · · · · · ·

On to Cochin in the southern state of Kerala. Women walk along the roadside balancing large loads upon their heads. On the waterfront catfish, just caught and still gasping, are laid out on display. Dragonflies hum through parks shaded by rain trees. Cruising the Keralan backwaters around Cochin the boat pushes through green clumps of water hyacinths, past banana plants and houseboats stitched out of bamboo and palm. Farmers and fishermen toil away in the heat as kids run alongside the boat, calling for me to throw them my pen as a gift to show off.

We dock at Coconut Lagoon, a riverside restaurant serving a vegetarian feast using banana leaves as plates. Encircling a mound of rice in the middle of each leaf is an assortment of curries and condiments (cabbage with grated coconut, beet with yoghurt, ginger chutney and lime pickle) to mix together with the rice and eat with the fingers – right hand only, please.

Masala dosa is my new favourite breakfast, a crisp pancake with curried potato hash and lentil-tamarind sauce. The sourdough flatbread *appam* is another speciality of Kerala state, leavened with *toddy*, a spirit made from fermented palm.

In Cochin we discover what a couple of the ethnic minority communities of the region eat. At her house, cooking teacher Nimmy Paul demonstrates the Syrian Christian food of her grandmother – recipes handed down for generations from mother to daughter, full with the fat, fragrant curry leaves from her garden. Over at Kodu House are the last vestiges of the Jewish cuisine of the area. It feels slightly odd to be in India and eating a Jewish meal of chicken soup with *matzo*-ish dumplings with chocolate pudding to follow – all of it endowed with a spicy local twist.

· · · · · · · · · ·

Dawn breaks over a rowboat upon the Ganges. It's full moon day at the Magh festival, which attracts pilgrims from all over the country to one of the world's oldest cities, Varanasi. Thousands of people are upon the steps lining the river banks, there to bathe and submerge themselves in the sacred water. A few of our group, more courageous than I, join them for a dip. That water looks very brown.

Holy men, hair matted in dreadlocks and some naked with their bodies covered in ash, camp out in makeshift tents. Residents, hawkers and curious backpackers mingle in a mass of colours. Bodies wrapped in white shrouds are carried to the shoreline and cremated on large piles of kindling, the ashes scattered. Dogs, cattle and goats nose through the rubble and monkeys move quickly across the building tops. It could be a scene from any age, except for the chirping of mobile phones. A *sadhu*, a holy man, gives me a blessing and dabs a circle of yellow and red clay between my eyes.

In the evening the same shores are packed again as the Ganges glitters with candles lit in memory of departed souls and set adrift to float away into the darkness. The moon throws a ribbon of orange across the black water. Cremations are going on in earnest now, and smoke from the many fires wafts into the sky as banked up corpses await their turn on the steps.

We travel by rickshaw *wallah* the following day to browse through Varanasi's markets, mazes of narrow lanes and bazaars where cows share space with humans and the ever-present monkeys peer from above to see what they might snatch. Cattle are revered here in India; they move freely and easily among the human populace and have right of way. Bumped from behind in the marketplace, I turn to meet the stolid expression of a cow, waiting for me to move aside.

After a visit to the buried Buddhist city of Sarnath, where the Buddha himself once came to preach, our van descends upon a village in the countryside with a small pickle-making factory. It is an arrival of aliens, true strangers in a strange land. Someone from another part of India might be an occasion here, let alone visitors like us. People climb onto rooftops to watch our approach. Kids run away in terror and hide, until curiosity gets the better of them and they peer around corners. Some of the group take their pictures with digital cameras and show them their images, and an hour later we have a laughing entourage waving us goodbye.

· · · · · · · · · ·

The Indian head wobble is a unique form of expression. As people fall into conversation heads begin to gently oscillate from side to side, seeming to show agreement and rapport, an unspoken communication of "I'm listening". If things turn confrontational or heated, the wobbling can become quite agitated.

In Delhi we sample *sattvic* Hindu vegetarian food, designed to keep one cool and calm and help promote "saintly character". No garlic or onions are used as they're thought to inflame the emotions. At a restaurant near the airport *tandoori* chicken, baked in a clay-and-cow-dung oven, is yellow and not the bright red I'm used to. That appealing crimson colour I like so much must be food dye.

Kebabs and luscious *biryani* – mutton chunks baked with rice and spice in a dough sealed pot – are on the menu at Dum Pukht at the Sheraton. Bukhara restaurant has *tandoori* cauliflower and *dal makhani*, slow-cooked black lentils enriched with plenty of butter and cream. Bustling Karim in Old Delhi's Muslim quarter dishes up tasty 'butter chicken' – bony bits of bird in a creamy tomato sauce.

Julie Sahni's nephew, a Delhi resident, suggests checking out *desi* Chinese food. Long before the term "fusion" came about, Chinese restaurateurs in India were adjusting their ingredients and spicing to suit the palates of their customers. Indian expatriates today reminisce fondly over the places they used to patronise in Delhi and Mumbai. The nephew recommends a spot.

Indian-Chinese may not improve on either cuisine, but it's an entertaining hybrid of Chicken Lollipops (deep-fried wings with meat scraped back along the bone to create miniature drumsticks) and *Gobi*

Manchurian (cauliflower florets meet a smoking-hot wok to create a texture of crunch around gooey, almost gelatinous innards). The fried rice is basmati. Main courses are stir-fried, thickened with cornstarch in the Chinese way.

No pork or beef here. Not much distinguishes the chicken and lamb Manchurians apart except the lamb's raw chillies, lurking like depth charges beneath the brown gravy. Tellicherry Chicken uses Tellicherry black peppercorns, considered by some the world's finest (Kuching back in Borneo would beg to differ, no doubt). This version tastes a bit musty, as if the pepper has been cracked too far in advance. Vegetarians are served by culture-straddling preparations of both Chinese tofu and the fresh Indian cheese *paneer*. For dessert the date pancakes might be the best bet, crisp triangles of pastry-wrapped fruit topped with candied walnut.

The next morning it's up in the predawn dark to stagger about, get dressed and board an early train from Delhi's busy station to Agra for the Taj Mahal. No doubt you've heard of it, seen the pictures, perhaps heard something of the Moghul ordering it built for his beloved queen after her death birthing their fourteenth child. I think about staying back at the hotel. It seems a bit of a touristy thing to do. But I do go, and am blown away by the Taj Mahal, stunning in its scale, awe-inspiring in its majestic presence and perfect symmetry. Sometimes it is OK to be a tourist.

. . . .

On the drive west to Jaipur in Rajasthan the landscape is a dusty green, with splotches of yellow from rapeseed fields and cattle dung stacked into artistic pyramids. Long-legged camels, topped with turban-clad riders, pass by, hauling carts laden with goods. Roadside businesses are just a chair or stool where customers drop by for a haircut or shave, a cup of tea or a manipulative session with the local bone setter. The van flirts every few minutes with head-on collision with oncoming buses crammed with people, additional overflow of passengers riding up on the roof. Peacocks perch in the trees on the approach to Jaipur as dark falls.

A swaying ascent on elephant back the following day leads up to Jaipur's Amber Fort, looking out over Rajasthan's desert plains (the spray from elephant snot makes a refreshing alternative to sunscreen). Afterwards, distracted by the dubious joys of Asian squat toilets, I wander dazedly out of a bathroom, leaving my hat and sunglasses in the stall. I head straight back inside to retrieve them. It's only been seconds but they're gone – back out under the blazing sun a man is making a beeline across the crowded square. Goodbye to all that. For a few rupees one of the ever-present vendors hands me replacements.

In the last few weeks the group has sampled Goan, Maharastran, Gujarati, Kashmiri, Punjabi and Mughlai cuisines, but has still only touched on the diversity of flavours out there in this fascinating country. Our time is up now – one last meal together. Quite a group they are, sitting around the long table:

Robyn, a Boston-based New Yorker who has had a rough few days after one wrong bite (unless it was that dip in the Ganges). India can do that to you.

Jill and Andy, Aussie expats who seem to share my view that doughnuts just may be proof of a higher power.

Writer and activist Phyllis from New York.

Ellen, losing her eyesight and travelling the world storing up images.

Long-time traveller Michael, who is building a house in Mexico.

Dorothy and her red shoes from Louisiana.

Carol, the 'Sweet Potato Queen' of Mississippi.

Carole of Portland, who has just come from touring Myanmar (Burma), where I'm headed next.

Terry, pastry chef from California – she won a gold medal at the Culinary Olympics a few years ago.

Jerry and Steven from Seattle – Jerry chef at one of the most acclaimed restaurants in the US.

And **Julie Sahni**, a lode of knowledge and experience. To have had someone of her stature in the culinary world leading the tour is – in a smaller foodie way, of course – rather like a member of a royal family offering you a personal tour of the castle's secret passageways.

The cooking here in Rajasthan has always lacked resources – fresh vegetables are hard to cultivate in this climate. Extensive use has developed of dried substitutes such as mango powder and lentils. Soup is made out of black pepper and soaked *poppadum* wafers. *Gotta*, dumplings of chick pea flour, replace meat or vegetables as the main star of a curry thick with yoghurt.

DAL (INDIAN LENTILS) & PILAU RICE

The lentil stew *dal* is an everyday staple of millions in India, eaten with rice or breads like *chapati* or *roti*. This *dal* is adapted from the recipe of my Anglo-Indian friend Des Peters, former fighter pilot from Madras and one of the best home cooks I know.

It's up to you as to how thick or thin you make your *dal*. I like mine quite thick, like a porridge, but many prefer it soupier. It's my understanding that *dal* in India would be teamed with plain white rice, rather than a flavoured rice like the *pilau* below. The combination works for me but you can just make white rice, or make the *pilau* by itself to serve with a curry or other main dish.

Serves 4. Approximate cooking time: 45 minutes

Dal:

1 cup (200 g or 7 ounces) red lentils, picked over carefully for any pebbles or debris

3 thin slices ginger, peeled

½ teaspoon turmeric (careful, it can stain)

1 teaspoon salt

3 tablespoons (45 ml) vegetable oil

8-10 curry leaves

1 small garlic clove, finely chopped

½ teaspoon black mustard seeds

½ teaspoon cumin seeds

¼ teaspoon cayenne

1½ tablespoon lemon juice (half a lemon)

3 tablespoons chopped fresh coriander (cilantro) leaves

Wash lentils in several changes of water until water is clear. Discard any floating lentils. Soak for 30 minutes and drain.

Place in a medium heavy-bottomed saucepan and cover with 3 cups (750 ml) water and add the ginger. Bring to a boil over high heat, skim well and add the turmeric. Lower heat and simmer, partially covered, until lentils are soft, about 30-40 minutes, stirring occasionally.

Scoop out a cup or so of lentils, mash them and stir back through the *dal* to thicken it. Add the salt and simmer uncovered another 5 minutes, or until thickened to your liking. Remove and discard the ginger.

Heat the oil in a small saucepan or frying pan on medium high heat. Add the curry leaves and cook for 10 seconds, scoop them out and add to lentils. Add the garlic to the oil and cook until golden brown, then remove and add to lentils. Add mustard and cumin seeds to the oil, cover the pot and fry until the mustard seeds "splutter" (sizzle and pop), about 30 seconds. Remove from the heat, stir in the cayenne, and pour the oil into lentils.

Add lemon juice and coriander leaves to the dal, stir in well and it's ready to serve.

Pilau rice:

2 cups (500 g) basmati rice

1 tablespoon butter or vegetable oil

6 cardamom pods

6 cloves

1 small cinnamon stick, broken in several pieces

Handful of curry leaves

1 teaspoon salt

Wash the rice in several changes of cold water, then leave to soak for 30 minutes covered in fresh cold water. Drain well.

Place a large heavy-bottomed saucepan on medium heat, add the butter or oil and the spices and cook 1 minute. Add the rice and stir until the grains are coated in the fat, then stir in 2½ cups (600 ml) water and the salt. Bring to the boil over high heat and then cover with a tight-fitting lid. Reduce the heat to low and cook for 15 minutes. Turn off the heat.

Let stand covered for 10 minutes, then fluff the rice up with a fork and serve. I like to pick out and discard the spices but they are traditionally left in, although not eaten.

BURMA

Myanmar, where women are women and men are men and both wear skirts, the long wraparound sarongs called *longyi*. The faces of females and children are daubed with a yellow paste made from tree bark that acts as a sunblock. The country is under military rule and is one of the poorest in Asia (shortly after my visit conditions will deteriorate still further through rioting, government crackdowns and a devastating cyclone).

Credit cards are not accepted anywhere except in a few upmarket hotels, which run them via Singapore and surcharge accordingly. ATMs are non-existent, so you need to arrive with enough cash to see you through your stay. The official government exchange rate to the US dollar is nearly two thirds lower than the black market rate, if changing it on the street, as I do.

Online access is controlled and many websites blocked altogether (although the genial young hosts of internet cafés will smuggle you in). The computers might not be working anyway - frequent blackouts and power failures mean telephone and electricity lines are often down in Burma; an eerie sensation in the smaller towns, completely in darkness until the generators kick in. All citizens must carry ID cards at all times with photo, thumb print and distinguishing features.

Yangon, formerly Rangoon, is lively and crowded, sidewalks teeming and trucks careering by so packed with bodies they look like an attempt on a world record. The huge Shwegadon Pagoda is of uncertain origin and age, the giant gold bell of its stupa the city's most prominent landmark. Two enormous white lions made of stone stand guard at the main entrance. There I shed my shoes and one of the monks shows me around the extensive grounds, the hot pavement scorching my wimpy bare feet.

· · · · · · · · · ·

North, by propeller plane, to Nyang-U, access point for Bagan (Pagan). The countryside is sunbaked green and yellow, with splashes of purple from bougainvilleas and everywhere the sugar palms that mean you are in South East Asia. At sunset, as the light starts to go, I climb one of the highest temples of Bagan, and look out across a plain dotted with thousands more of them erected in the eleventh and twelfth centuries. (With the addition these days, thanks to the unfortunate tastes of someone with influence, of the eyesore of a brand new building smack in the middle of them.)

I've already spent hours exploring the ruins, clambering in and over them and in one case underground into a monastery hollowed out from sandstone. A very good guide is with me, although he has a tendency to laugh hysterically at everything I say. Now I stay up on the temple steps, watching the view over Bagan until the sun is finally behind the hills and all its temples have disappeared into the dark. It's an image I'll file away with dawn recently on the ghats by the Ganges, and that same sun rising and falling over Cambodia's Angkor Wat years ago.

The next day it is a pleasure to be seated at the Green Elephant restaurant, in the shade of a bamboo tree with a cool breeze blowing up from the Irrawaddy River below. Fishermen work waist-deep in the water at the far shore. Smiling idly, I raise my cup to my lips - and splutter as I scald myself with boiling hot tea.

· · · · · · · · · ·

On the flight from Bagan via Mandalay to Heho, in southern Shan state, the earth below is a Martian red. It's another hour by bumpy bus ride along a potholed road to Nyaun Shwe township, the gateway to Inle Lake. Here Buddhist male monks are clad in dark red, while nuns and children have the same shaved heads but wear bright pink robes.

This has to be the first time I've ever checked into a hotel and been asked with concern "How much can you pay?" Later, asking for the bill after dinner at a nearby place, the response is "Up to you".

A hired boat with outboard motor and driver takes me out through the inland waters to the lake. Out under the vast sky fishermen row small boats with one leg on the oar in the local fashion. Villages have waterways instead of roads, the houses built on stilts. At floating markets long-necked Kayan women, rows of brass ringed around their throats, sell trinkets. There are floating gardens too, pinned into the lake bed, growing tomatoes and beans and garlic.

Lunch at a floating restaurant, with a young British woman I meet who's also travelling alone, is ethnic Shan food. At this meal this means different pork dishes: stir-fried with peppers, stewed in banana leaves or cooked down until dry and brittle. Shan style noodles, made of rice, have a satisfying chew.

· · · · · · · · · ·

"Even the rice tastes bad," said a backpacking friend who had travelled extensively in Burma in the nineties. Either I'm having better luck or times have changed. Back in Yangon I eat in restaurants targeted at tourists and well-heeled Burmese (a meal might run to several dollars), and also at local joints known to foreigners, although no concessions made for them. These are built with a roof and walls but no front, and you share your meal with the flies and mosquitoes that buzz about the diners.

Ordering is by looking and pointing - the couple of places that do have menus tend to be out of the interesting items on them anyway.

A plate of rice and a pot of weak tea appear on the table when you sit down, then you go and choose from what looks appealing of the prepared selection sitting out on display at room temperature.

Vegetables might include yellow beans topped with deep-fried shallots, or chopped straw mushrooms tossed with stringy greens and a kind of tofu made from chick pea flour. Salads come composed of fermented tea leaves with peanuts and raw garlic cloves, or crunchy roasted cauliflower florets with bean shoots and sesame seeds. All the salads have a pronounced pong - we are back in the lands of fishy condiments.

The chicken curry is all bones and the pork curry mostly lumps of fat, but their gravy is the thing. The basic Burmese curry, like its Indian counterpart, starts out with a base of onion fried slowly brown with ginger and garlic. Where the Indian cook might then add a shelf-load of spices, the Burmese cook does not, sprinkling in only some powdered turmeric root for colour and crushed dried chillies for mild heat. The thorough browning of the onion base and meat or veg gives the curry its own savoury roasted character, and on the table will be a saucer of pungent shrimp paste to dial up the flavour.

Everything is swimming in oil, perhaps as a form of preservative as the pots sit out all day in the heat. The idea seems to be scoop up from the bottom and try to leave a lot of the grease behind on the surface.

Yangon has a street of Muslim shops selling the rice dish that Indians call *biryani* and in Myanmar is also named *dan bauk*. At the entrance of each establishment are large tubs of saffron-streaked rice, embedded with a few scrawny chicken parts and dried raisins and cashews. Each serving comes with a side of sour mango pickle to add some punch.

And should you find yourself one day in Myanmar perusing a menu, a tip: "fried beating up egg" is scrambled, to you and me.

KYET THA SIPYAN (YELLOW CHICKEN)

The yellow refers to the turmeric in this dish although its final colour, at least when I make it, is more red-brown. If you don't want heat, omit the cayenne and increase the paprika to 2 teaspoons.

Serve with steamed jasmine rice and perhaps a home-made pickled cucumber salad (peeled, seeded and sliced cucumbers marinated briefly in a little vinegar and sugar).

Serves 4. Approximate cooking time: 1 hour to 1 hour 15 minutes

8 bone-in chicken thighs, total weight about 900g
(2 pounds), skin removed and discarded

½ teaspoon salt

¾ teaspoon turmeric (careful, it can stain)

1 large yellow onion, roughly chopped

2 cloves garlic

1.25 cm (½ inch) piece fresh ginger, peeled

2 tablespoons sunflower or vegetable oil

1½ teaspoons sweet paprika, preferably Hungarian

½ teaspoon cayenne

1 cup chopped tomato, fresh (if ripe - about 1 large
or 2 small tomatoes) or canned

2 tablespoons mushroom soy sauce or dark soy sauce

Fresh coriander (cilantro) leaves to garnish (optional)

Rub the chicken pieces all over with the salt and turmeric and set aside. In a food processor grind the onion, garlic and ginger to a smooth paste, scraping down the sides (if you don't have a processor, just chop everything as finely as possible).

Heat the oil in a medium-large heavy-bottomed pot over medium heat. Add the onion paste and cook, stirring often, until soft and deep golden-brown (add a splash of water if needed to prevent sticking). Cook until the water content in the paste evaporates and the oil separates out around the edges (the Burmese name for this curry translates to something like "Oil Returned").

Stir in the paprika and cayenne, and cook for a few seconds. Add the chicken, raise the heat to medium-high and fry, stirring and turning frequently, until the chicken is browned all over.

Add the soy sauce and tomato and 1 cup (250 ml) of water. Bring to a boil over high heat, reduce heat to low, cover the pot and simmer gently, stirring occasionally, for about 30-45 minutes until the chicken is tender (a knife blade will pierce through without resistance).

When the chicken is ready the sauce may be too thin and watery. If so, remove the chicken pieces to a platter and reserve. Over high heat, uncovered, reduce the liquid in the pot until it becomes a thickish gravy. Reunite with the chicken.

Serve garnished with the coriander leaves, if using. Better yet refrigerate the curry overnight and reheat to serve. (This will also give an opportunity to remove and discard some congealed fat from the top of the sauce, if you like).

Variation: Use 750 g (1 3/4 pounds) boneless skinless chicken thighs, each cut in half, and instead of water use 1 cup (250 ml) unsalted or low-sodium chicken stock, preferably homemade (see appendix).

PART TWO
EUROPE & NORTH AFRICA

9

UNITED KINGDOM

....,.................

From the window of the upstairs room at the Yew Tree, the washed ink skies and bare-branched trees in the green fields leave little doubt that winter has set in upon the land.

Marco Pierre White was the most influential British chef of the nineties. Acclaimed restaurants today from London to New York, Vancouver to Melbourne to Hong Kong are headed by cooks who came up through his kitchens. Retired from the stove himself but still a restaurateur, he has taken over the Yew Tree, a 17th century inn in the English village of Highclere, and turned it into an "eating and drinking house" (he detests the term "gastropub") featuring his greatest menu hits from over the years.

From the room it is only a few steps descent for breakfast, lunch and dinner and lunch again, stooping to avoid bumping my head on the low wooden beams. Marco can be seen popping in and out of the inn, either with his family or driver. Roast partridge comes "properly garnished", which means chestnuts, Brussels sprouts, freshly cooked potato chips, smoked streaky bacon, little chipolata sausages, watercress, bread sauce, fried breadcrumbs and roasting juices. The gamey-tasting bird (probably shot by Marco, a keen hunter) sits on a round of toast smeared with its mashed liver.

Quail eggs turn out to be a great match for finely minced *duxelle* of mushrooms and puff pastry, all brought together by a rich hollandaise sauce. More mushroom, as a soup whipped up into a frothy foam resembling cappuccino, and then pink slices of venison dressed with a bitter chocolate sauce. A crumble of flour, butter and sugar is strewn over tart apple and gooseberries (crumble, young man, crumble), and a boozy sherry trifle is served in a martini glass, at least an inch of cream poured over the top.

Marco's tastes in preparation and presentation are simpler these days from a heyday of French-inspired sauces and elaborate plating. "Mother Nature is the true artist", he tells me.

. . . .

To London: prohibitively expensive, grimy, grey, crowded, clouded - and one of the world's great cities, with the buzz that comes from being plugged into a centre of things. Around every other corner an ancient building or landmark or street evokes some sense of the past, half-remembered from movies, songs, and the Monopoly Board. (The names roll by - Piccadilly Circus, Berkeley Square, Marble Arch, Hyde Park...) History resides in the parks, the old pubs, the bookstores, even the Underground and the pigeons dotting the sides of the Thames.

The thin walls and sputtering showers of a bed and breakfast in the outer solar system of Edgware are my base for tripping around the city. Nearing Christmas the hotels are full and the main thoroughfares and stores of London congested with shoppers and tourists mingling under the festive lights, the streets dark by mid-afternoon and clogged with slow-moving black cabs and red double-decker buses. The wind cuts through my clothing - I'm rugged up like a Himalayan explorer while the hardy locals stroll by in T-shirts, perhaps donning a light jacket as a concession to the weather.

Sober broadsheets of current affairs are balanced by the tabloids; gossipy, salacious, reporting with relish on the scandal of the day. The broadsheets have pictures of prominent politicians – the tabloids take a different tack with scantily-clad - or simply unclad! - women sprinkled through their pages.

As in India, class can be a big deal here, although its importance has receded. Someone tells me that the finer restaurants are staffed with European waiters, as it might discomfort a Brit should their server's speech betray a posher upbringing than theirs. Is that it, or could something like hiring cheaper staff from abroad at minimal wage be more the issue?

At Wilton's behind the Ritz, doing business since 1742, eyebrows are imperceptibly raised at my Antipodean accent and casual attire, a jacket immediately produced from a discreet cupboard behind the front desk. Obsequious staff and waitresses in maid-like uniforms wait on the elderly blue-blood regulars who sweep in to dine on relics from the Anglo-French menu.

"Morning, Peters."

"Good to see you again, sir. Tom, do we have the Major's usual table ready?"

Over at Rules, London's oldest restaurant, the walls of the high, dark room are mounted with animal heads and framed pictures of people and places long past. At the Dorchester on Park Lane, Sunday lunch is fine but too stilted and hushed to enjoy properly, and in the bathroom an attendant, better dressed then you, is there to turn on the taps and hand you a towel.

· · · · · · · · · ·

"To eat well in England" declared author Somerset Maugham, "you should have breakfast three times a day."

Ordering a "Full English" anywhere brings a plate laden with fried egg, bacon, sausage, mushrooms, baked beans and grilled tomato, with the optional added weight of black pudding (blood sausage), triangles of fried bread or bubble and squeak, a potato and cabbage hash. The best breakfast I eat is at the Yew Tree, but the most memorable is at Bellucci's in London's working-class East End, a 'caff once notorious as hangout for 1960s gangsters the Kray twins. Surrounded by cockney-accented regulars straight out of central casting, my Full English is washed down with cups of sweet, milky tea and lungfuls of second-hand cigarette smoke.

British food is, for some, a synonym for abysmal quality. The old joke is that in Hell the cooks are English. Maybe the reputation was deserved once. Yes, plenty of the uninspired and lacklustre is still available in London, in quality not that far removed from the institutional. Beef in a stew at a celebrity chef's place has been carelessly trimmed so it's still way too fatty, the sauce one-dimensional and wan as if the meat has not been browned enough before braising. Waiting out there for the incautious diner are gluey gravies, vegetables cooked for approximately three years, and one encounter with a particularly indigestible rice pudding. The indifference extends to spelling errors on every menu I see, even in the high end places - a minor detail, but it does make you wonder if the lack of interest is carrying over into the kitchen.

But when it is on form - think of great joints of roasted animal (one day, slow baked Middle White pork with its meltingly tender meat, striations of fat and crisp crackled skin), surrounded with potatoes sizzled crisp in dripping, and if it's beef today also the puffy Yorkshire pudding. Mint sauce for lamb, apple for pig and gravy on everything. It's true that sometimes the gravy just seems to be margarine, flour and water boiled up with brown food colouring, with little taste and a gloopy consistency. But do I love it anyway and pour it over everything in sight? Of course! It's gravy!

Simpsons in the Strand, established 1828, is one venue that does right by the roast, the meats pushed around the dining room under large silver cloches and carved at the table. Here what passes for gravy is more refined and truer to the beast, an unthickened moat of its roasting juices. Dickens ate here, and Shaw, and Van Gogh (the website even lists Sherlock Holmes as a former guest). And now so have I.

Pies and pasties can be ordinary train station fare - or veer towards the artisanal when made by hand with crusts infused with suet (raw beef fat from around the kidneys). Custard is Britain's greatest contribution to the world of dessert sauces, its importance even acknowledged by the French – for whom British cookery normally a punchline - who call it *crème anglaise*. Many of the classic British puddings are custard based - bread and butter pudding, burnt cream aka *crème brulée* (origin claimed by Trinity College at Cambridge), lemon curd - and if not custard based, come with custard alongside anyway. Fascinating names, some of these "nursery puddings". Anyone for some Spotted Dick or Jam Roly-Poly?

When a change is needed from the bland, stodgy British fare - said as a fan - then you can always "go for an Indian". According to the newspaper one day London has more Indian restaurants than Bombay and Delhi combined, although most are really Bangladeshi run. Chicken Tikka Masala is considered a British national dish, as little eaten in India as 'spaghetti bolognese' is by Italians. Other multicultural options abound - an emerging trend for Malay and South East Asian eating houses is taking place in the streets around Charing Cross Road in the West End.

Another trend is for the "snout to tail" cooking exemplified by Fergus Henderson of St John restaurant, reclaiming offal and the lesser animal cuts for the British palate. At St John the plates are unadorned, minimalist, austere, expensive - but the bone marrow salad hits all its marks, roasted tubes of bone with a parsley and caper salad to relieve the richness.

At Le Gavroche its chef, Michel Roux Jr, sees me dining alone in the other corner of his restaurant and makes a beeline straight to my table to do his best to welcome me and make me feel at ease. I go for the classical French side of the menu which would have been in vogue in his father Albert's day, artichoke filled with chicken mousse and soufflé of apricots.

· · · · · · · · · ·

In the village of Bray, Heston Blumenthal, consistently voted in the world's top tier of chefs by his peers, pushes the boundaries of modernist cuisine at his Fat Duck restaurant. The tasting menu kicks off with a palate cleanser of lime, green tea and vodka frozen in seconds with liquid nitrogen. It continues with snail porridge, sardine sorbet and salmon enrobed in warm liquorice gel. Dessert does not get any less modern, with bacon-and-egg ice cream and orange jellies that turn out to be beetroot.

But at the Hind's Head pub Heston owns across the road, the bill of fare veers in the opposite direction to painstakingly-researched British food of the past: dandelion salad, Lancashire hotpot filled with lamb cubes and oysters. A revived, long forgotten 17th century dessert, Quaking Pudding, is a milky mousse that really does quake, or rather quiver. A steamed treacle sponge is so stickily saturated with golden syrup that it rolls right over my feeble resolve to eat only half of it, and is only lightened by pouring over the entire pitcher of double cream alongside.

· · · · · · · · · ·

Friday I travel up to Scotland by train, stopping off first to overnight at Sharrow Bay in England's Lake District and try their sticky toffee pudding. The original version of a dessert that has taken the world by storm is suitably decadent, steeped in its sauce for several days before serving, landing on the table drowned in butterscotch and cream.

I arrive in Edinburgh to spend a few days with friends Dave and Sarah, who are expecting their first child. With me is a second sticky toffee pudding, brought all the way from Sharrow Bay as a gift. Can I help it if they choose to have it one night while I'm still there?

Sheets of rain sweep the cobblestoned streets and lash about us as we forage around the town. Culinary local delights include the Deep-Fried Mars Bar. Edinburgh's fish and chip shops will batter and deep-fry anything desired or brought in, including but not limited to candy bars, pizza, pie and cake. Haggis - heart, liver and lungs boiled up in a sheep's stomach and paired with *neeps* (turnips) - looks intimidating but tastes like oaty meatloaf.

Sarah may be from Australia originally, but she shows she has a handle on Scottish cookery with a cracking meal of flaky-topped steak pie and *clapshot*, a creamy puree of root vegetables and nutmeg. Clapshot tastes like mashed potatoes that went travelling and gained life experience. I go to sleep warm and full, with the wind outside rattling the windowpanes.

SUNDAY ROAST - BELLY PORK

Really it should be roast beef here. There's a reason one nickname for the British is "beefeaters". Even the national dish of fish and chips tastes best when cooked in beef dripping, as they do in Yorkshire. But pork for me has to take the crown, with its burnished crackling.

Turn this into a proper British Sunday roast by serving it with all its classic accompaniments: roast potatoes, root vegetables and a green vegetable or two. Warm the plates to ensure everything stays hot. Gravy would be traditional, and I love it and a suggestion is below, but this roast should be so juicy that it's not really necessary. (Apple sauce is traditional too. To make your own peel, core and dice Granny Smith apples and cook gently in a small saucepan, covered, until you have a purée. Add a pinch of sugar and also a few drops of lemon juice, if you like).

Serves 4. Prepare ahead: Allow 24-48 hours to lightly cure the roast. Approximate cooking time: 3 hours including resting time.

2 kg (4½ pounds) piece of pork belly, bone-in and skin on, about 5cm (2½ inches) thick, ideally with a good layer of fat between skin and meat (ask butcher to score the skin - see below). Some chefs and butchers insist that female/sow pork tastes best.

Salt (see below)

1 teaspoon freshly ground black pepper

1 tablespoon olive or vegetable oil

2 onions, peeled and thickly sliced

One to two days ahead: If the butcher has not done this (and try to get them to do it, it's a lot easier and safer), score the skin in even finger-width lines with a box cutter or very sharp knife, without cutting into the meat below. Weigh the roast and measure out 1% of its weight in salt – so 20 grams salt (0.7 ounces) for a 2 kilogram (4½ pounds) roast, for example. (If measuring by volume rather than weight, calculate an amount of ¾ teaspoon of salt per pound.) Rub the pork all over with the salt and the pepper and refrigerate, uncovered. This will allow time for the salt to season the roast evenly all the way through, instead of just on the surface.

On the day of cooking, remove the pork from the fridge at least a couple of hours before to come towards room temperature. Preheat the oven to 160 C (320 F). Wipe the skin of the pork well with paper towels to remove any moisture, then rub the skin with the oil and sprinkle it lightly with a little additional salt. Line the onions in the bottom of a heavy-bottomed roasting pan and place the pork on top of the onions, skin-side up. Place in the oven for 2 hours. Fat should render off beneath the roast, but if your pig is lean and at any time the pan juices look like they are evaporating and burning, add a few tablespoons of water or wine to the bottom of the pan.

Raise the heat to 220 C (425 F) and cook for another 10-20 minutes or until the juices run clear when pierced and the skin has become crackling: golden brown, puffed and crusty. Remove pan from oven, transfer pork to a large platter and let rest in a warm place (such as near the stove) for 20 minutes. (If the crackling has not crisped enough, remove it by running a long-bladed knife around and underneath it. Place on a baking tray back in the oven while the pork is resting.)

If you have made gravy, add the juices that have pooled underneath the rested meat. Remove the crackling and chop it into rough squares. Carve the meat off the bone in one piece, then carve the pork against the grain into slices and serve with the crackling. The bones can be gnawed on later for any remaining meat.

GRAVY

Gravy is as British as Buckingham Palace, but this one also glances across the water for inspiration to France's classical Sauce Robert, served with pork and dating back to at least the 17th century. The acidity of the wine and mustard help balance the richness of the pork belly.

Serves 4. Approximate cooking time: 20 minutes.

1/3 cup (80 ml) dry white wine

1½ tablespoons flour

2 cups (500 ml) pork or chicken stock (see appendix)
or vegetable cooking water

Salt and freshly ground black pepper

1 teaspoon Dijon or grain mustard

Transfer the onions from the roasting pan to a saucepan. Spoon the clear fat out of the roasting pan and discard, leaving the darker-coloured meat juices behind in the pan (taste to make sure these meat juices haven't burnt, as this will make the gravy bitter. If they have, don't use them). Add the wine to the roasting pan and stir well to scrape up all the flavourful residue caramelised on the bottom.

Place the saucepan with the onions over medium heat. Sprinkle in the flour and cook, stirring, for a couple of minutes. Add the wine from the roasting pan and mix in. Add the stock or cooking water gradually to avoid creating lumps, stirring, then raise the heat to bring to a boil. Lower the heat again and simmer, stirring regularly, until the gravy has reduced to the consistency you like. Strain through a fine sieve into a smaller saucepan and discard the onions.

Add any juices from underneath the resting roast to the gravy. Stir in the mustard and salt and pepper to taste (you may not need any salt if the pan juices or stock are salty - or if too salty, dilute with a little water or stock). Reheat the gravy - don't boil it again after adding the mustard and juice from the pork, but do make sure it's hot.

Give it a good whisk, transfer to a warmed gravy boat or small jug and serve with the roast.

FRANCE

How sweet it is to be in Paris once again, by Eurostar under the water from London, and only minutes after arrival to be standing in the Gare Du Nord train station biting into a baguette and deciding on options for dinner.

Outside, reassuringly rude Parisians barge by on the narrow sidewalks. The Art Deco era 'Metropolitan' signs lead down into the depths of the underground subway, a great way to get around Paris and a more pleasant experience this time, after my previous visit in the height of summer (and a heat wave) revealed deodorant to be low on the list of French priorities.

Dusting off my high-school French, I'm once again surprised and pleased to find I can get by ordering a meal or booking a hotel for the night without resorting to English. Beyond that, my linguistic skills are a bit limited. I do know how to say perfectly "That is not a hat", but the situation has yet to arise where this might be useful.

I go to Notre Dame and Place de la Bastille, walk along the banks of the Seine and browse the open-air markets on the boulevards with their fresh produce. Poultry stands sell chicken and geese with heads and feet still attached. Many of the shoppers are dressed quite stylishly, especially the *grandes dames* in voluminous fur coats and carrying miniature poodles - pet as fashion accessory. Incredibly, there really are Frenchmen to be seen wearing berets and with long breadsticks tucked non-ironically under their arms. Green garbage trucks trawl the streets picking up the green trash bins, with green uniformed garbagemen armed with long green-brushed brooms.

Paris, as it has for centuries, has some of the heaviest hitters in contemporary gastronomy: currently names like Joël Robuchon, Alain Senderens and Alain Passard (and there's Alain Ducasse, and Alain Dutournier too – is being called Alain a head start in the French culinary scene?) Their grand dining establishments, flagships of these big guns of *haute cuisine*, mean meals accompanied by massive bills - several hundred dollars a head before the wine list is even looked at.

These temples can be chilly experiences, too. I have wanted to eat at Taillevent for many years, and their lunch menu is a fraction of the cost of dinner, but the snootiness of the staff makes for an uncomfortable couple of hours. From the moment I'm ushered in they look me up and down, with a particular focus on my shoes, and don't seem to like much what they see.

More inviting are Paris' *bistros* and *brasseries,* both the modern facing and the proudly retro. It would be cool to discover a new taste combination or two, but above all I want really good examples of the classics, dishes I've heard of or read about but never tasted - or perhaps *have* had before but never a decent, let alone definitive, version.

In some countries you can walk out of the front door, into the first eatery you find, and more than likely have a good meal. Japan is one; Singapore another. Before I had first been to France I assumed it would be too – in fact that it would probably lead the pack. I was wrong. After my first few disappointments, and standing outside a bistro after a particularly grisly and gristly steak *au poivre,* I realized a different approach was required.

Homework is needed, then. It might be all too easy to have a bad meal in Paris these days, but do a little planning and you eat very well. Like at lunch at L'Avant Gout, recommended by writer Jeffrey Steingarten, a small restaurant where you sit in elbow-bumping proximity with your neighbours. A croquette of deboned pigs' trotter and oyster mushroom precedes a piece of hanger veal topped with parsley pesto, vividly emerald. A molten-centred chocolate cupcake, oozing sauce, holds sway over vanilla ice cream and salted caramel butter. For cooking of this calibre, L'Avant Gout's menu is a bargain too.

Later, walking into Pierre Herme's pâtisserie in the sixth *arrondissement* is like entering a jewellery store, with its tiered displays of chocolates and macarons. "The Picasso of Pastry", Herme even has designer shows each year with catwalks and waiters-as models to show his creations. A *canele,* a pastry originally from Bordeaux, is flawless, crisp caramel shell enclosing a custardy, rum-laced core. Sampling the wares of Herme causes problems afterwards at the venerable Brasserie Bofinger, as it takes a valiant effort to consume a respectable enough amount of *choucroute garnie*, wine-braised sauerkraut piled high with various sausages and smoked and cured pork products.

The standout meal is at the miniscule bistro Le Comptoir. The chef, Yves Camdeborde, trained at the top restaurants of Paris and rose to the rank of assistant head chef at one, but instead of taking the top job chose to leave and open a no-frills spot serving fine dining quality at bistro prices. Half the price and twice as good as the competition, it became a sensation and led a revolution of other chefs falling over themselves to open their own smaller, cheaper places.

Dinner at Le Comptoir, Camdeborde's new restaurant, is one of Paris' toughest reservations. A request for a table, a month in advance, was met with a curt "We are always full, *monsieur.*" But no reservations are taken at lunch, and after loitering suspiciously around the entrance before service I snag a window table as soon as they throw open the doors. Moments later the place is jam-packed with customers.

The lunch menu rethinks the classics, but not in a fussy or contrived way. *Pot au feu*, normally a hot soup of miscellaneous beef cuts and vegetables, here becomes a slice of cold *terrine*, a jellied mosaic of the different meats with leek and carrot. *Boudin blanc* - a white sausage of pork and veal and cream made by the chef's brother

- is amazingly light textured. Plated alongside a glass jar of potato purée swimming in gravy, garnished with wedges of bibb lettuce, it's an ethereal "bangers and mash".

Then a *tarte tatin* turns up, an upside-down apple tart invented (probably) by the 19th century Tatin sisters and now popular around the globe. *Tatin* is one of those desserts I've never really 'got' as to why it's so popular, other than it's not the hardest dessert for a pastry chef to whip up. Le Comptoir's explains to me for the first time what all the fuss is about. The contrast of soft toffeed fruit and flaky, buttery pastry is fantastic, enhanced with a yellow dribble of custard and a scoop of fresh churned ice cream specked with the tiny seeds from vanilla beans.

· · · · · · · · · ·

A European rail pass doesn't quite get one to the village of Vonnas in the south of France, but from the nearest station of Bourg-en-Bresse it is only a short taxi ride through woods and past old farmhouses to the home of Georges Blanc Incorporated.

The Blanc family has run a restaurant in Vonnas since 1872. In 1968 the young Georges took over the business and embarked on an ambitious expansion of the modest roadhouse into a sprawl of restaurants, hotel rooms and shops, dominating the centre of town and these days its major financial driver. The food got a makeover too - rustic provincial cooking upgraded to *haute cuisine* of rare and expensive ingredients. The gamble paid off - Michelin guide's top rating of three stars was eventually earned and has been maintained ever since. The name and image of Georges Blanc is blazoned across everything in sight and for sale - cookbooks, kitchenware, portraits of Georges looking noble but inspired, tea towels, bathrobes, dustbins and umbrellas. Worryingly, a sign also points to Blanc-themed *lingerie*, but that turns out to be the French term for linen.

Next door to the main three-star restaurant (I glance at the menu

– the usual truffles and foie gras showered on everything) is the inexpensive L'Auberge Ancienne, which features Blanc family recipes. Especially luring has been word of the *poulet à la crème* made famous by the chef's grandmother. Outdated by today's dietary guidelines, the recipe (to serve four) calls for a chicken to be cut up and browned in about half a cup of butter, then a glass of wine and a quarter gallon of cream poured over and all allowed to bubble away until done. The chicken is a pedigreed *Poulet de Bresse*, the blue-legged local bird whose quality is strictly monitored.

Before reaching the main course of *poulet,* I must work through rich chicken liver pâté in brandy and then *quenelles de homard,* fluffy poached dumplings of lobster mousse smothered in a cream sauce. At last comes the chicken, predictably delicious. I had read that it's partnered with potato pancakes, but tonight it is basmati rice. Recalling a girl I once dated whose motto in life was "They can only say no" I ask, and the chef generously makes up a batch of pancakes for me at no extra charge. The pancake batter is enriched with clarified butter and cream, and the rice has a sizeable dollop of butter stirred through for good measure. My dairy and fat quotas for the next month have been filled.

. . . .

After taking the train west to Toulouse, first order of business is a trip to the laundromat, the hazard of travelling when you pack only a week's worth of clothes. Toulouse is a home of *cassoulet,* the French baked beans that arouse Gallic passions over what ingredients to use and how exactly to cook it. Heated arguments all the way up to blows have apocryphally taken place over issues such as whether or not to use breadcrumbs, and just which town in the area serves up the best.

I've read up quite a bit on *cassoulet* before coming. The Languedoc region bridges France's Mediterranean and South-West. Gastronomically, it's the bridge between the olive oil and tomatoes of

Provençal cooking and the cured meats and poultry fat of Gascony and the Basque country. Fats used around here are mainly goose fat, lard and olive oil, rather than butter. *Cassoulet* is a peasant dish, born out of poverty and necessity, and may have Spanish or Roman origins (stewing beans with fresh and preserved meat is common to many parts of Europe). The name comes from the earthenware pot, the *cassole*, in which it was traditionally cooked.

Despite many variations of the basic recipe, three towns in the Languedoc lay claim to being the Holy Trinity of *cassoulet* making. In Castelnaudary, generally regarded as the oldest version, the beans are combined with fresh pork, ham, sausage and pigskin. In Carcassonne mutton is added, and occasionally partridge. Here in Toulouse preserved goose or duck (*confit*) and the local sausage (*saucisse de Toulouse*) are also added to any or all of the above ingredients. A seafood *cassoulet* even exists, made with salt cod.

Although the presence of beans and meat are generally a given, every detail seems to inspire considerable debate. Should mutton even be used? Some feel it dominates the flavour of the other meats. Should the beans be fresh or dried? It's usually made with dried white haricot beans, but these didn't appear in France until the 16th century and were not common in *cassoulet* making until the 19th (originally fava or other fresh beans may have been used). Some contemporary chefs suggest using the Tarbais bean for a creamier texture. Are tomatoes a welcome addition? And if breadcrumbs are used, to make a crust, then controversy arises too over how many times - if at all - that crust should be broken while baking, some authorities stating seven or eight as the ideal number.

Happy to settle for merely a good example while in Cassoulet Country, and hopefully avoid getting in a fistfight with anyone over how authentic it is, an hour after getting to Toulouse I'm seated at the table in Chez Emile, fork and spoon in hand and appetite in stomach. Emile's *cassoulet* is a pot of white Tarbais beans, oven cooked with tomato, garlic, herbs, several kinds of sausage, a leg of duck *confit* and clumps of pigskin and pork fat. After all the fuss it tastes like... really good baked beans. And no-one has punched me.

· · · · · · · · · · ·

"*C'est rare*" ("that's unusual") says a silver-haired woman, pleased when I offer her a seat on the crowded Metro. Back in Paris, a bistro a block from the Seine has *coq au vin*, cockerel in red wine, one of the classics. There are warning signs - multilingual menus, a room full not of locals but nonplussed tourists and surly waiters, and, most ominous of all, an enthusiastic endorsement in one of the major guidebooks. The *coq* is sad indeed, the bird boring and the flavours in the greasy sauce muddy.

The morning after it's ice cream for breakfast, justified by staying close by the famous Berthillon, *glace* makers in the Ile Saint-Louis since 1954. Concerned it's crossing an invisible line to be eating ice cream this early, I try to imagine milk on cereal as I nibble on a small cone of liquorice. It's all dairy, right? As for a scoop of mandarin sorbet - fruit to start the day, what could be more virtuous?

CRÈME GLACE A LA VANILLE (VANILLA ICE CREAM)

French ice cream is a frozen sauce. It's *crème anglaise*, 'English cream', the custard we met back in England, churned into a solid state.

You need an ice cream machine for best results, and there are some good and inexpensive brands. (If you're like me, you'll go through a phase of making every flavour of ice cream you can think of or dream up, and then the machine will gather dust in the cupboard for the next year.)

French sauces are about technique and can be tricky to master at first, especially the ones involving eggs. It's worth persevering because, once you have a feel for it, you have a whole range of custard or ice cream ideas you can play around with. And a good thing about homemade ice cream is that you know exactly what's in it.

The egg yolks are lightly cooked, so be conscious of this if serving to anyone who would avoid raw eggs. The unused whites can be frozen for another use.

Vanilla has come to mean, says the dictionary, "having no special or extra features; ordinary or standard". That seems unfair on a flavour derived from the fruit of an exotic orchid, in its true form the second most expensive spice after saffron.

Serves 4. Approximate cooking time: 45 minutes, including infusion time

1 cup (250 ml) whole milk

1/8 teaspoon (a pinch) salt

1 cup (250 ml) heavy (double) cream, divided

4 large egg yolks

½ cup (100g) sugar

1 vanilla pod (bean), split in half and the little black seeds inside scraped out into the sugar

In a medium saucepan on high heat bring milk, salt and ¾ cup (185 ml) cream just to a boil with the vanilla bean. Remove from the heat, cover and let stand for 30 minutes to infuse the vanilla flavour.

In a medium bowl, whisk egg yolks and sugar together until pale and thick.

Reheat the infused milk to just below boiling. Add a little hot milk to the yolks to temper them, whisking all the while, then add this mixture back into the milk. Place the saucepan over medium low heat and stir constantly until the custard thickens to the consistency of heavy cream, and a line drawn down the back of the stirring spoon stays in place. Don't take this too far, or you will end up with sweet scrambled egg instead of ice cream! As soon as the custard is thick enough remove from heat and add the reserved cream to help cool it and stop it overcooking.

Strain the custard through a fine-mesh sieve into a bowl set over ice water and stir continuously for 1-2 minutes. (Some cooks like to rinse and dry the strained vanilla beans and store in a jar of sugar to flavour it.) Once cooled, refrigerate the custard until very cold, then churn in an ice cream machine following the manufacturer's instructions. At this point it will be like soft-serve ice cream – transfer to the freezer to harden fully. Remove from freezer and refrigerate 30 minutes before serving.

Variations: Instead of the vanilla bean you can infuse other flavourings into the custard. You could make almost any flavor of ice cream you want - here are just a few of the possibilities:

Pistachio

Commercial pistachio usually doesn't have any pistachio at all in it. A high-end brand might contain 5% if you're lucky. It is really almond extract and green food colouring.

Use 200 g (7 ounces - about 2 cups) shelled unsalted nuts. Toast half of them briefly in a dry frying pan or on a baking tray in a moderate oven for 5-10 minutes, then combine with the raw nuts and rub off the skins in a tea towel (dish cloth). Grind in a food processor with some of the sugar and a few drops of the cream to make a paste, and use in place of the vanilla bean. Leave the nuts in the finished ice cream, or after infusing in the warm custard strain them out for a smoother texture.

Cinnamon

Infuse one cinnamon stick in the milk in place of the vanilla bean (plus you can add a pinch of the ground spice to the sugar, if you like).

"Secret Formula"

(approximates the flavor profile of a well-known soft drink)

Infuse zest of one lemon, a small vanilla bean and half a cinnamon stick in the milk.

Mint

Infuse a bunch of fresh peppermint (about 1 packed cup) in the milk.

Peach

Use only ¼ cup (50 g) sugar when making the custard. Pit and dice 4 large, ripe peaches. Cook with ¾ cup (150 g) sugar and juice of one lemon for about 30 minutes over medium heat, stirring often, until it becomes a jam. Stir this into the warm custard, infuse for 30 minutes, then strain the custard through a fine-mesh sieve and chill.

SPAIN & PORTUGAL

Sleeper carriage? This one has been more of a sleepless carriage. In the six-berth cabin overnight to Madrid the man below, when not consumed with coughing fits, is on his mobile phone. The other occupants are snoring away tremendously. I am then fined in the middle of the night for not having the right stamp in my rail pass, despite having shown it at the station before boarding the train.

Emerging grumpy and less than refreshed into the sunlight, I find today's newspaper claiming Spaniards to be the least stressed of European citizens. No one seems in too much of a hurry in a large, pleasant city, its wide boulevards and narrow medieval-width side streets filled with pedestrians. The sky is blue and the sun out but the temperature hovers just above freezing. Outdoor public art is everywhere, statues and modern sculptures mounted in the parks and squares. Not far off Gran Via, the main drag, is the Almudena Cathedral, and next door the huge Palacio Royal. The guards strutting about the palace wear hats that look like a back-to-front baseball cap crossed with a plastic flower pot.

Sooner or later most countries have worked out that fried pastry is a Good Thing. In Spain any time is a fine time for *churros con chocolate*, filling the void for breakfast or a wee small hours snack. At San Gines in the old quarter, servers snip lengths off ridged coils of extruded dough, all crunch and grease, not sweet at all until dunked in a steaming cup of the cinnamon infused, toothpaste-thick hot chocolate.

Having heard about a larger type of *churro* called *porras*, I ask for directions to a Bar Madileno, which apparently does them.

"Bar?"

"Bar."

"Bar?"

"Yes, bar. *Bar.*"

"Ah. Barrrr."

If you are more used to Latin American Spanish, the original in Spain takes some getting used to, especially the lisping of "s" pronounced as "th". One story has it that a King Ferdinand had a speech impediment and the courtiers imitated it to appease him, the populace followed and it snowballed from there.

Museo del Jamon, "Museum Of Ham", is the kind of museum a gourmand appreciates - to enter the delicatessen is to be confronted with hundreds of legs of pork hung across the walls, layered vertically row upon row like guitars in a music shop. The logical next step is to sample a selection of the raw ham, cured with salt and age. *Serrano* is the basic *jamon* and *iberico* a grade higher, made from pigs fatted on black acorn. *Jamon de Bellota* is the really good stuff, a carefully-cured haunch of free range animal, sweeter, more nuanced and complex with flavours of cheese and nut. Slices of *chorizo*, the paprika-spiked sausage, go well too with the hunks of dry bread at hand.

Fast Good is a groovy, postmodern space of green and white with plastic counters and round stools and tables – the sort of place the Jetsons might go for lunch. Video screens are built into the walls and the bathrooms light automatically as you approach them. At this hamburger joint of celebrated chef Ferran Adria the meat patties are well seasoned and really juicy, but contain bits of gristle and connective tissue that catch in the teeth. Of two burgers requested cooked medium, one is raw inside and the other well-done.

In lieu of a milkshake they proffer a fantastic lime and yoghurt drink, but the fries are a disappointment. They may have been proudly cooked in Spanish olive oil, but the end result is just soggy and would not pass muster at any of the large fast food chains. I like a crisp fry - if you bend it, it should think about snapping. "We spent eight months on the French fries" Adria is reported as saying. "We were about ready to kill ourselves." I would have been OK with a few casualties if it meant my potatoes were crispy.

....

From the large train windows the Spanish countryside flashes past - a rocky landscape cut by a few rivers, grazing cattle or goats and the occasional hilltop castle. In Seville the traffic-jammed roads are lined with orange trees and buildings of faded yellow. Sanlucca is an outlying neighbourhood of white Mediterranean houses, slowly patrolled by grandmothers in black. This is the location of Hacienda Benazuza, the El Bulli Hotel. Time to get a better sense of what Ferran Adria's crew can do.

Every year up to half a million people try for a table at Adria's El Bulli restaurant in northern Spain, and only eight thousand will be successful (the restaurant is open only April until September each year). But the "Dali of the kitchen" has now opened a hotel in Seville with a restaurant that serves El Bulli's "greatest hits" from over the years. And scoring a reservation here was surprisingly easy.

While El Bulli is the current owner of Hacienda Benazusa, the original building itself is ancient, over a thousand years old and home over the centuries to Saracens, Moors, kings and noblemen; a fantasy of courtyards and sweeping staircases, patios and landscaped gardens. In the high-ceilinged restaurant El Bulli's original recipes are recreated, each listed on the menu with the year of its invention. A boutique choice from a "water list" is poured by a white-gloved waiter and kept chilled in a bucket tableside.

What follows is a trip to a culinary circus, an illusionist's stage show of gels, hot airs and foams, boundary-stretching textures and flavours - dubbed by some "molecular gastronomy" (although not by

Adria, Heston Blumenthal and the others who cook this type of food). Twenty-seven courses are served, consisting of just a few bites or even one bite. Some are wonderful; some are just interesting.

They arrive in a constant stream, sometimes several plates at once. Fried whole baby prawns, the size of a pinky nail, are heaped in a paper cone and dusted with dried lemon zest. An "olive" looks like one but isn't, instead it's a thin, fragile green membrane encasing a liquid olive essence. Freeze-dried corn powder is topped with lime jelly pearls, and a corn mousse with truffle juice and cubes of foie gras; a caramelized tomato comes encased in transparent sugar "glass". A skewer of cauliflower and raspberries sprinkled with flakes of sea salt is weird, but it works. A tube contains an extract made from shrimp heads to be sucked out with a straw, while "crazy salad" has the components of a traditional salad turned into gelatins, emulsions, powders and squiggles of mousse.

Lettuce is grilled. Chicken wings are deboned, formed into squares and crisped, plated with tandoori foam and oyster cream on a sticky puddle of reduced poultry cooking juices. "Kellogg's Paella" is a packet of dried saffron rice, like yellow Rice Krispies, to be poured into a cup of hot fish soup to reconstitute. Finally *petit fours* are placed down, little candies of chocolate and nougat, to sweeten the bill.

Having reached the hacienda before midday, and being over-excited about being here, I have made the mistake of sitting for both lunch and dinner, variations on the same menu, so have essentially eaten the same extensive tasting twice in a day. That's over fifty dishes, plus an impromptu between-meal snack of aged *jamon* at the adjoining cafe. By the time those second and last *petit fours* appear in the evening I'm extremely uncomfortable - and a formidable breakfast is still to come in the morning.

....

Leaving the sun behind in Seville, in the thirty minutes it takes by rail up to Cordoba the sky clouds over and rain is spotting the ground. In mid-afternoon the walled old city centre is deserted except for a few cooing pigeons. *Siesta* time - outside the major cities shops close in the middle of the day, perhaps meaning for the worker a leisurely lunch with a nap to follow. From about two to five in the evening the crooked streets remain empty. As it grows dark, things gradually stir to life - a few tourists moving about and ladies of the night beckoning them from darkened doorways.

In the city centre accommodation is cheap and clean and just a few steps away from the Great Mosque. Constructed in the eighth century, the largest site of Muslim worship in Europe was converted into a Catholic church some four hundred years later, so it has a cathedral set in the middle of it. At ten o' clock on Sunday the bells ring out, summoning everyone to Mass.

A Spaniard will not sit down to dinner until ten or eleven at night and be still going past midnight. At 9.15 one night it's already as late as my stomach can stand and I turn up at a *bodega*, a wine and tapas bar, definitely pushing my friendship with the waiters by being there so early. My soup is slammed down in front of me. Slopping over the side of the bowl is *salmorojo*, a cold puréed liquid of tomatoes, garlic, olive oil and day-old bread – a thick Andalusian gazpacho - garnished with diced *jamon* and hard-boiled quails' eggs. An unusual dessert follows, of orange sorbet with cubes of gelled Pedro Ximenez sherry and a generous slick of olive oil. The dessert manages to arrive mostly still within the plate.

· · · · · · · · · ·

Paella has awed me as an exotic and alluring dish ever since, as a kid, I saw a picture in a cookbook - gleaming yellow rice loaded with chicken, red sausage, mussels and shrimp. But my first *paella* in Madrid was horrible - stale, lukewarm grains tasting of old fish and tinted with artificial food dye. Instead of the imagined abundance of meat and seafood there were a few bullock bones and whiskery prawn shells.

Most recently there was El Bulli Hotel's deconstructed, dehydrated version. I need a chance at a proper *paella*, and that is why I am pulling up a chair at La Matandera, an old farmhouse among the rice fields of Lake Albufera outside Valencia. The seventy-something farmer-turned-restaurateur cooks, over a wood fire, what's reputed to be one of the best. It's made from scratch, so a long wait follows - a bowl of mushroom soup and a blood sausage quiche are brought to stave off any hunger pangs.

The finished *paella* is presented in its large black iron pan (a *paelleria)*, with towels wrapped around the handles so the customers don't brand themselves. No seafood in this ultra-traditional version - the short grained *bomba* rice has been simmered together with duck, chicken, rabbit, rosemary-purged snails in the shell, both white and green beans and a few pinches of saffron threads. Despite the shopping list of ingredients, the rice remains very much the star. It's a relief to finally experience a true *paella Valencia*, and my inner child thanks me, although in truth it is overly oily for my tastes and the pieces of assorted meat are tough.

· · · · · · · · · ·

On to Barcelona, stopping first in Alicante on the eastern coast with its impressive fortress of Castillo Santa Barbera above the town. The view from the summit in one direction displays the rooftops of Alicante, and in the other lazy circles of seagulls over the blue sea. Between trains I find quick time for some shrimp, grilled *a plancha* on a heavy iron plate.

Throughout the trip I have been lining up outside restaurants the way other people might queue for exhibitions or theatre tickets. Cal Pep in Barcelona takes this to a new level. After a long wait in a line outside, the early birds snatch seats at the tapas bar as soon as they open. Before the food has even started arriving, a jam of people is already squeezed into the narrow lunchroom, packed in directly behind those of us perched on the stools. We eat our lunch with impatient eyes boring into our backs, seats filled again the second they are vacated.

The tapas here are seafood based, overseen by the raspy-voiced Pep behind the bar as master of ceremonies. The diners eat whatever Pep and his cohorts place in front of us - whole sardines floured and fried, calamari with chickpeas, and clams in a buttery sauce strong on garlic.

Really good house-made bread starts dinner later at the Basque restaurant Gorria, useful for sopping up an appetiser of *morcilla*, blood sausage padded with rice. *Pochas de Sanguesa* may be the perfect legume dish, a soupy stew of white beans with bits of bacon and ham. A portion of suckling pig roasted in herbs and white wine has the skin as crisp as you always wish it would be. A square of fried custard, and the waitress flirting gently with me, and all is well with the world.

....

Lisbon gets going late. Midnights it is humming but by mid mornings the city still feels hung over, just a few souls raking leaves in the gardens and fishermen casting their baits on the banks of Rio Tejo. With its hilly streets and cable cars the sprawling city could be an ancient San Francisco. A giant Christ the Redeemer statue stands, a counterpart to the even larger one in Rio in Brazil, Portugal's former colony.

Written Portuguese resembles Spanish, but the spoken language is very different, sounding to these untrained ears like Russian spoken by a Scot. When one isn't paying attention some of the conversations seem remarkably like English phrases that make no sense. Walking along, you might overhear a snippet that sounds something like "Afternoon, Sam. Cabin bruises?"

Lisbonites start their day with a cigarette, a pastry and a shot of strong coffee. Having eaten Portuguese-inspired egg tarts in Manila and Macau, it seems reasonable to start off my sojourn in Lisbon with a visit to Pasteis de Belem, whose tarts are baked from the original recipe of a nearby monastery. Not exactly off the beaten path, it's necessary to squeeze through a throng of Japanese tourists to get to the bar and order a crinkly-skinned *pasteis de nata* (and then return and order a second one minus the cinnamon sugar topping - purely for analysis, of course).

In the window of a nondescript bakery on a cobblestoned side street are more sweet bites, little fritters called *sonhos* - "dreams" - made of fried *pâté a choux* dough. Irregularly shaped, light, eggy and slightly chewy, they are even good cold, a rare thing to say about any fritter.

The eating is good in Lisbon, both in and out of the tourist haunts and in places that range from homely to hip. Vegetable soups are thickened with potato. Rice is baked with shredded duck meat and slices of red *chouriço* sausage glowing with paprika. *Ahheira* is another sausage, this one yellowish, made out of different meats bound with bread. Dried beans, soaked overnight before cooking, feature in many of the dishes.

Portuguese cuisine, like Spanish, has made its mark around the world. Extensive colonists, the Portuguese heavily influenced the cooking of Goa, Macau, Brazil, Mozambique and Hawaii. Ideas from the former colonies have also returned back to the tiny motherland. At Pap restaurant, stew "Azores style" stars large pieces of beef, spoon tender, the braising sauce a rich reduction of wine vinegar, onions, garlic and bay.

On my last night in Lisbon I go to hear *fado*, Portuguese blues, in a restaurant in the old Barrio Alto. In the candle and lantern-lit room a procession of male and female singers run through laments in sad minor keys, accompanied by instruments including the twelve-string Portuguese guitar. Plenty of tourists are in the room but about half the crowd are regulars, swaying and singing passionately along with the songs.

FABADA (WHITE BEAN AND CHORIZO STEW)

Beans are very popular in Spanish and Portuguese cooking and in their former colonies – Mexico's *frijoles*, Brazil's *feijoada* – where the use of white beans gives way to black or pinto.

Instead of using the dried beans you could substitute two 440 gram (15.5 ounce) cans of beans, drained of their liquid, and just add those to the sautéed onion and tomato and heat through. It would certainly be quicker. But it's not the same – in canned beans there's a slight sliminess that I find unappealing.

Serves 4. Approximate cooking time: 3 hours, including soaking time

225 g (8 ounces) dried white beans, such as haricot, cannellini or Great Northern (about 1 cup)

1 bay leaf

2-3 garlic cloves

225 g (8 ounces) Spanish-style dry chorizo (about two sausages), half left whole and the other half sliced in rounds or diced into cubes

1 tablespoon olive oil

1 small onion, finely chopped

1 celery stalk, finely chopped (optional)

1 tomato, peeled and diced

½ teaspoon freshly ground black pepper

Salt

2 tablespoons fresh flat leaf parsley or chervil, chopped

Pick beans over carefully for any debris or pebbles, then wash well. Place in a medium-sized saucepan and add boiling water to cover by 5 cm (2 inches). Leave uncovered for 1 hour. Drain in a colander and rinse.

Place beans back in the saucepan and add cold water to cover by 2½ cm (1 inch). Bring to a boil over high heat and skim off any foam, then add the garlic, bay leaf and the piece of chorizo you kept whole. Lower the heat to medium low and simmer gently, uncovered, until tender, 1-2 hours. (If you cook them at too high a heat they can split). Stir regularly and add water as needed to keep beans covered by 1 cm (½ inch) liquid. Skim off excess foam now and then. Depending on the age and size of the beans, they may take 2 hours or more to become tender.

Turn off the heat and remove the bay leaf and chorizo. Discard the bay leaf and slice the chorizo. Scoop out about 1½ cups of beans and mash them (or purée in a blender or food processor for a smoother texture) and stir back through the rest of the beans to thicken them, along with the sliced chorizo.

In a small frying pan over medium heat, heat the oil and cook the remaining sliced/diced chorizo until it is crisping and rendering out its fat. Add the onion, celery and tomato and sauté until softened and the onion translucent. Bring the pot of beans back to a gentle simmer. Add the contents of the frying pan to the beans (including the fat) with the pepper, and cook for another 10 minutes.

Taste and add salt if needed - you may need ½ teaspoon or so. Stir in the herbs and serve.

Variation: Use a 115 g (4 ounce) piece of bacon, smoked pork belly or ham, cooked with the beans then shredded, and 115 g (4 ounces) chorizo, sliced or diced and cooked with the onion and tomato.

ITALY

"As they ate, they spoke of eating, as always happens in Italy" -
Andrea Camilleri

First stop in Italia is Genoa, an old seaport with a vaguely menacing air. It has been home since 1780 to the shop Romanengo, makers of candied fruit. Strawberries, peaches, apricots, plums, melons and figs are soaked repeatedly in syrups for several weeks until the water content in the fruit has been replaced by sugar. Romanengo keep the final results on the shelves for only two weeks, as no preservatives are used and the flavours start to fade.

Candied fruit, also known as crystallized or glacé fruit, brings childhood memories of my notoriously sweet-toothed grandfather candying figs, or of nibbling through my grandmother's dense Christmas cake hoping to strike the bits of them dispersed inside it. A once-a-year treat, expensive glazed jewels, sweet and translucent, candied fruit seemed to a seven-year-old the ultimate of luxury.

As an adult the trouble is that often the commercial product does not taste much of the actual fruit, and it is like eating coloured sugar. The friendly woman behind the counter at Romanengo makes up a box of one of every kind for me in their hard sugar shells, the fruit weeping a sticky liquor when bitten into. A bite of the fig - which really tastes of fig - and I am a kid again in the backyard of my grandparents' house, my grandfather picking a ripe specimen from his tree and explaining the start of the candying process to me.

In Italian food, as eaten in Italy, good ingredients are key, with an emphasis on only three or four flavours in a dish. Sauces for pasta may just be fresh tomato and olive oil, or melted butter infused with sage leaves. Nor is black pepper ground over everything; the cliché in other countries of the Italian waiter with an enormous pepper mill not a reality here. (At one restaurant in Italy I'm familiar with, black pepper is offered with exactly one pasta dish - and that is a once-a-week special.)

In Genoa and its province of Liguria the star is pesto. I try the blended sauce of raw basil, garlic, pine nuts and olive oil several ways: layered with sheets of fresh pasta, tossed together with a chewy, spiral shaped noodle named *trofiette* and stirred by the dollop through bowls of minestrone soup.

....

Most tourists just pass through Bologna as they commute between Venice and Florence. They are missing one of the culinary highlights of Europe. Emilia-Romagna, Bologna's province, is the home of *ragù Bolognese; parmigiano* cheese (the real Parmesan); balsamic vinegar; cured meats like *prosciutto, mortadella* and various *salumi*; pastas such as *lasagna, tagliatelle, tortelli, tortellini, tortelloni*; and the rice dish that was everywhere in the Nineties, *risotto*. What do these all have in common, besides their point of origin? Most are known around the world in versions that often bear scant resemblance to the original.

Known as *Bologna La Grassa* (The Fat) for its indulgent cuisine, Bologna has a well preserved medieval centre of rust-coloured arches and columned walkways, with a church, tower or square every few blocks. (Another nickname, *La Rossa* - the Red – refers to the colour of those porticos and also its left-leaning politics.) For centuries a base of learning and the arts, it has Europe's oldest university.

One-upping Pisa, two leaning towers recline just off the main square. The local populace seem to spend their free time strolling the ochre streets. *Bellissima* girls nip around on mopeds. Cafés are full of Italians gesticulating excitedly at one another. On every other street corner couples are making out, one pair both holding burning cigarettes carefully aloft.

Given just flour with egg (here in the north) or water (in the south), the Italian character has expressed itself with hundreds of shapes and sizes of *pasta*. To move town to town, even just a few miles, is to find new variations. Chengdu back in China may have had the noodle dish "ants climbing a tree", but in Bologna you can begin your meal with *strozzapreti* - "priest stranglers".

In the Emilia Romagna area they make their pasta by hand, rolling it out with a large wooden pin until it is thin enough to read newspaper print underneath. This manual method is rare even in the rest of Italy, where a wringer-like machine is used to roll out the dough. The yolks of the local eggs used are a fierce orange, making the pasta golden enough that chefs in some other countries resort to adding saffron to mimic the hue.

· · · · · · · · · ·

Picture a white bowl. Inside it is a tangle of bright yellow ribbon pasta. Clinging to the strands are nubbins of meat and vegetable that have braised slowly over hours down into a dark red-brown mass. A fine dusting of *parmigiano* cheese tops all.

Meet *tagliatelle al ragù*, pasta with Bolognese sauce. The original version of what the Brits call "spag bol" (although never paired with spaghetti here) is one of the world's great taste sensations. I have to restrain myself from ordering it at every meal.

When I walk into Trattoria Meloncello on the Via Saragozza just outside Bologna's city centre, about to order my seventh or eighth bowl of *tagliatelle al ragù*, I don't know yet that I am about to find what I have been searching for. Meloncello's *ragù* is not liquid at all, soft clumps of meat with a little orange oil, extremely savoury, verging on salty and too intense to eat by itself without mixing into the *tagliatelle* underneath. Only a couple of tablespoons of *ragù* top a small bowl of pasta, and it looks unlikely to be a big enough portion, but it's so rich that on finishing it one feels sated.

"*Prego*" says the waiter, checking in as I finish scraping my plate to see if I want something to follow.

I wave emotionally at the bowl. "It's so good!"

"Of course" he says, not the least bit surprised. "It is the best!"

The structure of a full-blown Italian meal is *antipasti* (appetisers), *primi* (pasta, rice or soup), *secondi* (main of meat or fish), *contorni* (vegetable side dishes) and - for those who can still manage it by then - *dolci* (sweets). I don't know how many eat that way that often, but I did meet a Tuscan businessman once whose wife's great pleasure was to prepare such a meal every single evening. He would have a salad for lunch.

Antipasto can include cured meats – lunch at the very old delicatessen Tamburini has *felino* salami ("cat", but it's pork) and another salami made out of goose that is pretty assertive. "Gamey" would be putting it mildly. Mains are usually simply prepared; pork loin cooked in milk, guinea fowl roasted with sprigs of rosemary. Serving sizes are restrained, and there can be a heavy hand with the salt. The side vegetables cost extra, as does bread – you pay a "bread charge" when you sit down in a restaurant, whether you eat any of it or not.

The one real disappointment in Bologna is when I stray from the casual family-run *trattorie*, which I always like to imagine have elderly *nonne* (grandmothers) in their kitchens, and dine at a *ristorante* whose (male) chef has applied Frenchified technique to the local fare. Heavy sauces cloak already rich dishes, along with unnecessary garnishes and tricked up presentations. It is like seeing kids dressed up in their Sunday best, stiff and uncomfortable, when you know they'd be much happier running around in regular clothes.

Italian sweets are not the cuisine's strongest point, with one exception. After or between meals is a good time to stop by one of the *gelaterias* dotting the city, as long as they have a sign posted of *produzione propria* - made in-house. *Gelato* is churned to have less air than ice cream, making it denser and more flavourful. It is hard to beat the simple *crema* of vanilla and lemon, but my favourite is the pale green pistachio. Today, a cone of sour cherry is making a strong case for consideration.

. . . .

I push out beyond the city into regional Emilia Romagna. In Polesine, in the lowlands some forty kilometres from Parma, is one of the prized delicacies in Italian gastronomy. *Culatello* is king in this part of the Po Valley. While *prosciutto* is made from the whole leg of the pig, *culatello* is made from the boned-out rump, sacrificing the rest of the meat (perhaps I shouldn't say sacrificed, as the trimmings are ground up to make an especially appealing salami). This "super prosciutto", rarer and commanding a higher price, ran foul of modern health inspectors and the traditional method of production nearly died out, but it's seen a recent revival of fortunes with the involvement of Slow Food Italy.

Massimo Spigaroli, chef-owner of Al Cavallino Bianco and president of the *culatello* association, gives me a tour of the cellar where the lute-like hams are quietly aging. Before lunch I walk along the riverbank, the crunch of gravel underfoot, birdsong and the distant hum of traffic the only sounds.

In the dining room Spigaroli presents paper-thin slices of *culatello* aged eighteen, twenty-four and thirty-six months respectively, the taste darkening with age. No figs or melon or other pairings here to compete with the purity of the ham – just bread and butter. The onslaught of food continues with *tortelli* – the local name for ravioli - of spinach and *parmigiano,* and then *stracotto* (pot roast) with polenta. Stopping there would have made the perfect lunch, but an assent to dessert induces a coma-like nap on the train to Parma.

In Parma the eleventh-century cathedral has a sixteenth-century fresco by Correggio that is as extraordinary a work of art as I've seen.

The dome of the cathedral is a painted swirl of angels, hundreds of them spiralling round and round, ascending ever upwards until they fall up into the heavens of the ceiling high above. As often happens, Correggio's efforts weren't that appreciated during his lifetime. He died unaware that his work would one day be a major drawcard for the tourist hordes.

The real reason for the visit is food of course - the city's two most famous edible products of *parmigiano* (parmesan cheese) and *prosciutto di Parma*, raw cured ham. Both are made to specific regulations and strictly controlled conditions to ensure quality. It has a cycle to it - the whey from the cheesemaking is fed to the pigs whose fate is to be made into *prosciutti*.

At a dairy where the cheeses are made the cows are housed nearby, beneath a sort of massage machine which they can activate to scratch their backs. I'm not sure what purpose it serves other than pleasure, but one cow remains backed up into it and won't let any of the others near, her eyes bulging each time the machine hits the right spot.

At *prosciutto* producer Pio Tosini it's equally fascinating to stand in and under a forest of meat, in a cellar hung with thousands of lard-coated hams that will age two or three years. *Il Maestro* - the master curer - tests when a ham is ready by sliding a horse-bone needle into the meat in several places and holding it under his nose.

In foggy Modena I visit one of the leading producers of *balsamico di Modena*, artisanal balsamic vinegar, and taste recent vintages as well as vinegars aged for twelve and twenty-five years. The producer has an adjacent restaurant open for lunch, and to say he's strict is an understatement. His terse response to an appeal for black pepper: "We last served that in 1971".

My friend Alessandra meets me for dinner at Modena's modernist leaning La Fransecana, with its five different textures of *parmigiano* as mousse, foam, sauce, souffle and crisp wafer. The meat for the *tagliatelle al ragù* here is cooked with the water bath technique sous-vide for ten hours, and hand shredded rather than minced. A very modern approach, a twenty-first century take on the dish, but it doesn't banish memories of Meloncello. It's my birthday, and Alessandra's gift is a bottle of fifty-year-old *balsamico*. This is the magic stuff – it enhances everything from meat to cheese to berries and is even good drizzled sparingly over ice cream. It should never be poured, but doled out by the teaspoon.

Alessandra is working the next day, so I go solo for a lunch that is the opposite experience of forward-thinking Fransecana. In the back room of a seventeenth-century delicatessen, a few tables comprise Hosteria Giusti. The food is traditional and tremendous, especially their sheer *tagliatelle* draped with *guanciale*, cured pig cheek. I don't order *tagliatelle al ragù* for the simple reason it isn't offered on the menu. If it had been, it would have been my fourteenth.

••••••••••

North. In the mountains of Piedmont, cheese makers are at work. Their damp cellars, deep underground, hold wooden benches lined with cheeses covered in furry white and green moulds, exuding an ammonia that clogs the nostrils and stings the eyes. It produces more apprehension than anticipation about lunch, but the cheese turns out to be quite mild.

Turin, Piedmont's capital, might be underrated by tourists the way Bologna is. Constellations of stars and planets are corded up in lights along the wider thoroughfares, above fountains and coloured street lanterns. Con Calma in the outskirts has feathery *gnocchi* in a pool of melted *raschera* cheese. A real skill, to make lumps of mashed potato and flour seem light! Cambio in the town centre is a grand old restaurant with such Piedmontese classics as *grissini* (bread sticks) and *carne cruda*, raw veal sausage. If you're being served raw meat, there's somehow more confidence in a place with chandeliers. It suggests they're not skimping on quality.

The pasta in Piedmont is the richest in Italy, containing up to forty egg yolks per kilo of flour. *Agnolotti*, the local ravioli made from this dough, are more delicate than the filled pastas of Emilia Romagna. The same dough can be turned into the thin angel hair pasta *tajarin*, at this time of year – winter - its most esteemed topping simply butter and shavings of raw white truffle priced by the gram.

Yes, white truffle is in season in northern Italy, and the odiferous fungi sell for up to four thousand Euros a kilo. Local hunters use trained dogs to sniff them out before bringing the specimens to market or conducting clandestine deals in car parks. I confess to not being the biggest fan - they are just too... truffly for me, with a scent somewhere between raw garlic and a ruptured gas main. (Although perhaps not the stinkiest foodstuff – the Asian fruit durian was once described as like eating custard while standing over an open sewer).

. . . .

Medieval knights errant had their quests for grails and what not. Mine's for the perfect *risotto* and it takes me to the small restaurant Da Mino, in the town of Robbio in the rice-growing region of northern Lombardy. I board the wrong train from Milan and have to double back and then change buses, making a flustered arrival just in time for lunch. No English spoken here and no menu - the husband runs the front of house while his wife toils away in the back in the kitchen. Like that *paella* back in Spain, and unlike most professional kitchens where they parcook their *risotto* ahead of time, here it is made from scratch.

Diners are plied with a flow of appetisers over the forty-odd minutes it takes to make the risotto, a stream of stuffed eggplant rolls, vegetable-topped *bruschetta* and *lardo*, thin slices of pure pork fat accented with rosemary. My anticipation is building and building until finally, with a flourish, the main course is presented - and it is *tagliatelle* pasta with seafood. After all the trouble to get here, risotto isn't on today!

Dismayed, I ask the host, "Risotto?"

"No, no", he says, misunderstanding, thinking I have my terminology mixed up. "T-a-g-l-i-a-telle."

Somehow we manage to communicate a bit more. He invites me to come back the next day (although I almost get that wrong too, mistaking *domani* for Sunday, *Domenica*, when instead it means 'tomorrow'). His wife makes the risotto, toothsome grains swollen with stock and filled out with sausage and cannellini beans. Good as it is, somehow I feel the quest continues, and that still out there somewhere is the Ultimate Risotto...

• • • • • • • • • •

Have many places been invaded more often than Sicily? Over the centuries each passing seafaring power seems to have felt a sudden urge to pop ashore and overthrow whoever else was running the show at the time. The Greeks, Romans, Vandals, Byzantines, Phoenicians, Arabs and Spanish all came, each new wave leaving its mark on the island and on the cuisine.

Sweets and sharps predominate in the flavours, vinegar balanced by sugar, fruit next to meat. I don't know which of the conquerors contributed to the legacy of ice cream sandwiches for breakfast, but gelato inside brioche buns is a popular way to start the day. Who am I to argue with that? (And anyway, after Berthillon in Paris I'm an old hand at this sort of thing.)

In Palermo the outdoor markets feature giant whole swordfish with their rapier snouts intact, and plenty of tuna (bluefin - the Sicilians don't seem to mind too much that it's endangered). In the Spirit of Adventure I eat a spleen sandwich from a street cart vendor. Corruption is still rife, the Mafia very much active, and the local restaurants have to pay them protection money. I dine at a restaurant which has been reported as defying this – it is nearly empty and police cars are parked outside. It doesn't feel like a meal to linger over.

At a cafe in Noto, a few hours' drive from Palermo, they're trying a bit hard to be modern. First course is clams and mussels in a tomato broth - topped with strawberry gelato and olive oil sorbet. Ingredients prepared with skill, co-existing awkwardly in the same bowl. Ice cream for breakfast as a tradition, OK, but ice cream with fish? It's a dish that should come tagged with a creativity warning.

RISOTTO AGLI ASPARAGI (RISOTTO OF ASPARAGUS)

Make a memorable risotto in the comfort of your own kitchen – no ticket to Italy required. Don't use the wrong kind of rice, as I did the first time I tried to make it, or you'll end up with a bowl of mush.

Serves 2. Approximate cooking time: 45 minutes.

225 g (8 ounces) asparagus

4 cups (1 litre) chicken stock (see appendix) or vegetable stock

4 tablespoons (60 g) butter, divided

1 small onion or half a medium onion, finely chopped

Salt

1 cup carnaroli or arborio rice

1/3 cup (80 ml) dry white wine or dry vermouth (optional)

1/2 - 3/4 cup (50 g – 75 g) freshly grated Parmigiano-Reggiano
or Grana Padano cheese

Freshly ground black pepper

Juice of 1/4 lemon (about two teaspoons)

Snap the woody ends off the asparagus and add to the stock to flavour it. Separate the tips from the stalks, and finely chop the stalks into rounds.

Bring the stock and asparagus ends to a boil in a medium

saucepan over high heat. Add the asparagus tips and cook for about 1 minute until crisp-tender. Turn off the heat, remove the tips with a slotted spoon and run cold water over them, then drain them well and reserve.

Heat half the butter in a heavy saucepan over medium low heat and cook the onion with a pinch of salt until soft and translucent but not coloured, about 10 minutes. Remove and discard the woody ends from the stock and bring it back to almost a gentle simmer - hot but not boiling.

Add the rice and chopped asparagus stalks to the onion, raise heat to medium and cook for 2-3 minutes, stirring. The rice should become translucent around the edges but don't let it brown.

Add a ladleful (about ½ cup) of stock to the rice - there should be a loud sizzle - and stir until absorbed. Add the wine now, if using, and reduce until absorbed, then another ladle of stock and let that absorb.

Keep adding stock one ladleful at a time and stirring frequently just until the rice is almost "al dente" (soft but still with a little bite) and the risotto is creamy but not runny, about 20 minutes. You may not need all the stock or, if the rice is thirsty and you run out before it's ready, use hot water. Add the reserved asparagus tips and warm through for a minute.

Beat in the cheese, remaining butter, lemon juice and salt and pepper to taste (if you have used commercial stock you may not need to add any salt). If the risotto seems a little thick by now, beat in a couple of tablespoons more hot stock to loosen it. Remove from heat, cover and let stand a couple of minutes for everything to meld. Serve immediately in heated shallow bowls.

AUSTRIA

From Italy to Vienna by train, heading up through the Austrian Alps and Innsbruck. Here are the winter wonderlands of rooftops dusted as if by icing sugar, lakes of ice and white-capped mountains carpeted with pines. Bridges run across deep ravines as northward the countryside becomes greener, willows lining rivers and houses scattered halfway up hillsides laced with vineyards. At each stop people pile out for a cigarette.

Austria - land of lederhosen, Freud and Strauss, but more importantly for some of us also *schnitzel*, goulash and tennis-ball-sized dumplings. German is what's spoken here. Let's compare some words for "cream" in a few European languages:

Italian - "*Crema*". Let that roll across your tongue.

Similarly in French – "*Crème*".

Then Spanish - "Crema"again.

And German - "*Schlag*" (whipped cream).

The fried pastries those other countries call *bomboloni*, *beignets* or *boules* become *Krapfen*. Pork - *porc, maiale, cerdo* - is now *Schweinefleisch*, "swine flesh".

The papers recently reported a population crisis of declining birth rates in Europe. Maybe that's not the case in Austria - in Vienna prams and young mothers are everywhere and some days of the mild winter are positively balmy, great for walking. Statues, palaces and monuments are a reminder of the glory days of the Austro-Hungarian Empire. Bicycle lanes run between the roads and sidewalk and the tourist who wanders onto them is in danger of being ironed flat as an Austrian pancake by a speeding cyclist. Passers-by greet each other with "*Grüss Gott*" - "God says Hi" - the local way to say hello.

Viennese cuisine's greatest hits are imports from that heyday of imperial expansion. More on the Big Two, *schnitzel* and goulash, later. The strudel and cakes in the Viennese cafes originate from Hungary. (The first of those cafés supposedly began with a hoard of captured Turkish coffee beans.) Other foods can be traced back to Poland, the Slavic states or Bohemia (now the Czech Republic). Beyond these influences the cooking resembles that of its larger neighbour Germany - hearty rib-sticking stuff of meat, potatoes, pickled cabbage and dumplings.

The omnipresent dumplings come many ways here. *Spaetzle* are small egg drops extruded into boiling water until they float to the top, ready for a baptism in browned butter. *Semmelknoedel*, another standard accompaniment for braises or roasts, is a single, large bread dumpling. Dessert time brings *topfenknodel*, sweet cheese dumplings coated in breadcrumbs and served with stewed apricots or other fruit.

It all sounds very heavy, but the dumplings have all been carefully made and are fluffily light in texture (except that bread dumpling, which is pure stodge). Another starch, potatoes, seems fairly inescapable too. In a meal at old school tavern Bein Czack they turn up in the first course, main course, and added in to the mixed side salad.

Over a few days I cover the classics: *tapelspitz* (boiled beef with dill), *grostl* (a hash-like fryup of leftovers), and *backhendl* (VFC - Viennese Fried Chicken, served with lemon wedges wrapped in muslin to prevent unseemly pips). *Wurst* stands are everywhere, the sausages griddled hot-dog-like and thrust into hollowed-out bread rolls with a squirt of hot mustard or sauce. (I try one. What's the *wurst* that can happen?) *Leberkäse* translates as "liver cheese", but is a pork product that traditionally contains neither.

On the sweeter side are strudel, *palatschinken* (crêpes rolled up with a jam filling), *powidtaschl* (pastry pumped full of plum jam) and *kaiserschmarren*, "emperor's mess", a thick omelette torn into shreds with rum-soaked raisins and cherry compôte.

··········

Wiener schnitzel ranks high in the pantheon of breaded, fried meats. It may be adapted from the *costoletta* of Milan, although contention exists over just who borrowed from whom. Several sources have it that Figlmuller is the place to go in Vienna for *Wiener schnitzel*, although an Austrian in Vietnam had warned "it is for tourists".

Figlmuller's *schnitzel* is enormous, overlapping an already sizeable plate, over half a pound of white veal beaten out flat, dredged first in flour, run through beaten egg and fine breadcrumbs and immersed in hot fat until crisp and golden. Impressive dimensions, virtually greaseless (the writer Joseph Wechsberg said you should be able to sit on one without staining your trousers), but rather dry. With it comes a vinegary salad of lettuce plus waxy potato slices dribbled with dark green Styrian pumpkinseed oil.

I have read that a true *schnitzelmeister* shakes the pan during cooking to create steam and puff the crust away from the meat, blowing the *schnitzel* up like a balloon. Figlmuller's however is thin and the breading firmly adheres to the veal. In search of the answer I tirelessly consume further *schnitzels* around town, but never find the one that hits all the right notes of big and puffy and juicy.

··········

In Austria, *Gulasch* - goulash - is a stew. In Hungary, where it originates from, *gulyás* instead refers to a paprika soup, and the stew would be more properly called *porkolt*, or *paprikash* with the addition of soured cream. All clear on that? In a Hungarian restaurant in Vancouver once I ordered *porkolt* - I must have pronounced it exactly correctly as the waiter looked down at me and said "Oh, you're Hungarian."

"No," I smiled.

"You are," he insisted, and nothing I or my girlfriend said could dissuade him.

Perhaps he was right, since paprika does seem to really warm my soul, especially the Hungarian kind (the taste is of the Veal Paprika my aunt Jenny used to make when I was a child). I don't know of another nation that elevates a single spice to the level at which Hungarians venerate paprika.

Near Vienna's Mak Cathedral I slip into a small bistro to try goulash, Austrian style. The menu is untranslated from the German but this looks like the right spot as a number of menu items end in "*gulasch*". I pick one at random and point to the word. The solemn, moustachioed waiter shakes his head. "*Nein.*"

I try again, but he stands firm.

"*Nein.* It iss not for you."

Am I not worthy? Some sort of membership is needed in Vienna to order a bowl of stew? Taken aback, I'm doing my best to muster some outrage when he attempts to explain, running out of anatomy phrases and using his hands. What I've been trying to order is an offal goulash, loaded with lung and possibly other unspeakables. More bizarre things have crossed my palate in recent times but, suddenly moved he's doing his utmost to steer a naïve tourist in the right direction, I let him guide me to the wild mushroom one.

Moments after slipping into a seat at the bar at the hip new Österreicher am Mak, and placing my order, a waitress appears and sets before me a packet of cigarettes and matches. A new trend in appetiser I am as yet unaware of? I even check the package to see if it is edible, some El Bulli-like molecular gastronomy inside joke. It turns out my request in my very best German for *Gulasch* has been heard as *gauloise*, a French brand of smokes. Misunderstanding corrected, access to the veal goulash is granted, here redolent with hot paprika, marjoram and caraway.

· · · · · · · · · ·

Westward to Salzburg, where it is too warm for snow but is drizzling lightly. My hotel is in the grungy area around the railway station, but across the river the old part of the city looks beautiful, if a little kitschy. Over that way is Peterkeller, which claims to be the oldest restaurant in Europe. Their Continental menu is undistinguished, but for dessert is there any real choice for a tourist but the famed Salzburger Nockerln? Raspberry purée hides beneath three scoops of marshmallowy baked meringue, moulded to look like the hills that surround the city. Peterkeller's version tastes like they may have used vanillin (derived from wood pulp) rather than the true, more expensive, vanilla.

On the way back to the hotel (where *The Sound of Music* plays round the clock on the TV) I lose my way and pull out my map to consult. It doesn't help much as it is of Vienna - I have thrown away the wrong one.

PALATSCHINKEN (PANCAKES)

These pancakes are simple and sweet and are like a comforting hug from an Austrian grandmother (I think - I don't actually know any Austrian grandmothers). The usual way they were served to me in Austria was spread with good jam and rolled up. I also like them sprinkled with granulated sugar and then a lemon wedge squeezed over the sugar to dissolve it into a syrup.

I once made the perfect pancake at a friend's place – a thing of beauty. Feeling confident and wanting to show off, I flipped it instead of turning with a spatula. It landed on the floor beside the stove and was immediately devoured by her dog.

Serves 2. Prepare ahead: Rest the batter for one hour up to overnight. Approximate cooking time: 10 minutes.

Scant 1 cup (125 g) flour

1/8 teaspoon (a pinch) of salt

2 large eggs

1¼ cups (300 ml) milk

1 tablespoon (15 g) butter, melted in a pan over low heat until a light brown colour, plus additional butter or oil for greasing the pan

Sift flour and salt in a large bowl and make a well in the centre. Add the eggs into the well and whisk the mixture well to combine. Add a quarter of the milk and whisk until it becomes a smooth paste, then add the rest of the milk slowly, whisking until blended and the consistency of thin pouring cream. Strain through a fine sieve if there are any lumps.

Rest for one hour at room temperature, or in the refrigerator for two hours up to overnight, tightly covered. Stir in the melted butter just before cooking. (If batter has become too thick after resting, thin again with a little extra milk or water.)

Heat a 25 cm (10 inch) skillet or frying pan, preferably non-stick or well-seasoned through use, over medium-high heat. Grease lightly with butter or oil. Pour about ¼ cup (60 ml) of batter into the pan. Swirl to evenly cover the bottom. Cook until the pancake is browned on the bottom and then turn (or if you dare, try flipping!) to cook the other side. Repeat.

Serve pancakes with jam or with sugar and lemon wedges.

ICELAND

I saw a puffin today - on my plate. Sorry about that. I tried whale too, served as a bloody-tasting sashimi. When in Rome – or in this case, Reykjavik... once is enough for both.

The Icelandic landscape is unlike anywhere else; perhaps parts of the Scottish Highlands the closest comparison. It is otherworldly - barren and largely treeless, and at this time of year cloaked in snow and ice.

The weather isn't too bad, although it can change several times in a day. Driving from the capital Reykjavik out to the large Langjokull glacier, and up onto it on an open air vehicle, the passengers are lashed with the rain and stinging hail. I'm wrapped in several layers plus a blanket to keep warm, my sunglasses also coming in handy to protect my face. The glacier face around us is vast, but visibility is restricted to just a few metres.

On the way out we have passed through Geysir, the original gusher that gave its name to all the world's other geysers, and on the way back stop at Gullfoss, a partly frozen waterfall outside Reykjavik. Iceland has several active volcanoes too, burbling away ominously in the countryside, threatening one day to rain fire down upon the island's inhabitants. Driving or walking outside the urban areas, one often happens across strange stone formations in the middle of nowhere, and who knows just who might have put them there - this is a land of trolls and goblins.

Beneath my hotel is a museum of archaeological remains from the

Viking period. The nearby weekend flea market is not too exciting for the tourist, mainly old clothes and second-hand CDs. Reykjavik in winter is blues, greens and greys, a grim sky over timbered buildings that huddle next to the teal sea. The town centre is fairly small, and can be walked around in a few hours including restorative stops for coffee and waffles. More than half of Iceland's population of three hundred thousand live here in the capital.

Up one of the hills, off the main shopping street of Laugavegur, is the house-turned-museum of sculptor Ásmundur Sveinsson, creator of phantasmagorical science fiction-like works. In the garden, soaring, strange-limbed creatures look eyelessly out over the city.

· · · · · · · · · ·

Wednesday starts off with a visit to a hot pot, an outside communal bath. The naturally heated pools have varying temperatures - the submerged part of the bather is toasty and warm while any exposed areas are simultaneously experiencing the cold and rain. After a dip in each of the pools, the sauna room is the final stop before a shower and the change back into street clothes. The largest and most tourist-frequented of the hot pots is the Blue Lagoon spa, 45 minutes' drive from Reykjavik, but the town itself has smaller public baths for the locals.

The same thermal energy that heats the hot pots provides free natural hot water for everyone. The waters may be pure but they carry a sulphurous odour, off-putting to those who are not used to it. A glass of tap water for drinking is much smellier than its counterparts in other countries.

Although this is the time of year to see the Northern Lights, the overcast weather hampers any chances of doing so. I head out with my friend Erna in the dead of night and freezing temperatures, driving out beyond any city lights to maximize opportunity and visibility, standing outside for as long as I dare and then ducking back into the car for snatches of warmth. When we do glimpse the aurora at last it is just a green smudge behind some clouds. At least I can say I saw it.

Going to the movies is a cheap and popular pastime, especially when the temperature drops. An Icelandic quirk is the insertion of an intermission arbitrarily into the middle of each film. The first time it happens I'm absorbed in a bad Hollywood potboiler when mid-scene the picture suddenly stops and the lights come on. I think the projector must have broken down, but everyone is calmly heading out to the lobby for popcorn and drink refills, then filing back to their seats. A few minutes later the action resumes.

Icelandic is the closest modern language to Old Norse, the tongue of the Vikings, and would be quite difficult to learn, but I don't meet anyone without a good command of English. Nearly all family names end in "son" or "dottir" after the father's name. You might meet a Karl Jonsson (son of Jon) or be introduced to his sister Margrét Jonsdottir.

Eating out is ruinously expensive, even with the recently-devalued kroner, and the quality can be spotty. One of the best value restaurants in Reykjavik – and for me one of the best here at any budget - is Icelandic Fish & Chips, an organic bistro near the harbour co-owned by journalist Erna Kaaber and US author and TV personality David Rosengarten.

I've eaten my share of fish and chips around the globe, especially in the UK, but Icelandic Fish and Chips is the best yet. In their health-aware take the batter for the fish is made out of spelt rather than refined white flour. It is cooked in olive oil, and the chips are baked, not fried, with the skins left on. The fish is impeccably fresh, my favourite the ling cod with its melting texture. Instead of mayonnaise the tartare sauces are made from *skyr*, a yoghurt-like fresh cheese. Erna's mother makes up vats of tasty soup for starters, unstinting with the cream, so one doesn't have to worry about the overall meal being too low fat.

Icelandic lobster - which is really langoustine or giant prawn - is awesome, so sweet, great as a bisque-like soup. A place outside Reykjavik serves them in the shell, sautéed in garlic butter and accompanied by freshly-dug potatoes. The local lamb is very good too, both as a roast dinner and smoked in sandwiches. A Sunday dinner at

Erna's family home features an unusual cut of lamb, skin crisp like Peking duck, and roast potatoes glazed in sugar in the Danish fashion (a good percentage of the population are descendants of settlers from Denmark).

More ways with fish: the local version of surf and turf is a combination of fish - cod, say - with melted lamb drippings. Sushi and sashimi seem to be in vogue these days with Icelanders, and why not when the raw product is this good. Graflax is sugar-cured salmon, fragrant with dill, shaved into translucent pink wafers to top buttered black bread.

Food was also traditionally preserved by burying it (someone mentions this was because salt wasn't available to the original inhabitants, although thinking this over later makes me wonder why they didn't just evaporate seawater). The fermentations that follow with this process can be a challenge for the modern visitor. With reluctance I try the notorious *hákarl*, "rotten shark". I try to swallow, but have to spit it out – the taste is pure ammonia - and conceding defeat, rinse out my mouth with the schnapps called *Brennevin* or "Black Death". I'm sure it was invented just to kill the taste of that shark. On the agenda still to come, at this traditional feast at Viking Village, are pickled ram's testicles and jellied sheep's head. Authentically recreated foodstuffs, or a hilarious joke on the foreigners? Who would voluntarily eat this stuff, except out of necessity?

Reykjavik has an energetic night life, its cafés and bars full of debates, jazz, and enthusiastic drinkers. It's a cultural place too, with a thriving arts scene and an international film festival. A late-night bite after clubbing often takes place at the famous hot dog stand Baejarins Beztu, where you can order a *pylsur*, or lamb hot dog. Tacked on the wall is a clipping of former US president Clinton contentedly polishing off one. I keep running into pictures of him in restaurants on my travels around the world. That guy sure got around in his day.

GRAFLAX (CURED SALMON)

Originating in Scandinavia and popular in Iceland, this cured fish makes a great starter. One of my favourite ways to serve it is as a finger food teamed with the guacamole recipe from the Mexico chapter (cured or raw salmon and avocado have a real affinity). On little crackers or squares of dried bread, place a thin slice of *graflax* and top with a small dollop of guacamole.

You'll need a set of scales for this recipe to ensure the right amounts of salt and sugar for the cure.

Serves 4 as an appetiser.
Approximate preparation time: 48 hours.

2 teaspoons black peppercorns and 1 teaspoon coriander seeds, or 2 teaspoons freshly grated lemon zest (zest of 1 organic or unwaxed lemon)

35 g (1.25 ounces) sea salt

35 g (1.25 ounces) sugar

500 g (1.1 pounds) sashimi-grade salmon fillet, centre-cut (preferably the same thickness all the way through, to cure evenly), skin-on

1 tablespoon (15 ml) akvavit (Danish caraway-infused spirit) or zubrówka (Polish bison grass vodka) (optional)

1/3 cup fresh dill

Toast the peppercorns and coriander seeds in a small dry frying pan over low heat for a few minutes, until the coriander seeds darken slightly and smell aromatic. Cool, and grind to a coarse powder with a spice grinder or mortar and pestle. Combine spices with the salt and sugar in a small bowl (or if using the lemon zest instead of the spices, add this now).

Remove the pinbones from the salmon, if this has not already been done by the fishmonger. These are all the row of little bones that need to be pulled out gently with tweezers or needlenose pliers. Use your fingers to feel for where they are.

Place a long square of foil on the kitchen counter, large enough for wrapping the salmon. Spread a piece of plastic wrap (cling film) the same size on top of the foil. Sprinkle about a quarter of the salt and sugar mix on the wrap in the middle, in an area about the size of the salmon. Place the salmon on top, skin side down, and sprinkle the remaining mix all over the salmon flesh evenly. Wrap up tightly with the plastic wrap, and then the foil to make a parcel. Place the parcel in a bowl (there can be leakage) and refrigerate for 24 hours.

Unwrap the salmon, rinse briefly under cold running water to remove any remaining cure, and pat dry well with paper towels. Rub with the aquavit or vodka, if using. Cover with the dill and rewrap in fresh plastic wrap and foil. Place on a tray. Place another tray or board on top, and weigh it down with bottled or canned goods. Return to the refrigerator overnight.

When ready to serve, unwrap the salmon and scrape away and discard most of the dill (don't worry about a few pieces still sticking to the salmon flesh). To serve, slice the flesh as thinly as possible with a sharp knife on a diagonal angle, leaving the skin behind (which you don't eat). If not confident in your knife skills to slice thinly, instead dice the salmon as finely as you can Refrigerate any left-over *graflax*, and eat within a day or so.

TURKEY

At eight o clock in the morning the wail of the *muezzin* is calling fellow Muslims to prayer. Muslims pray to Mecca five times a day, the truly devout rising in the middle of the night for an additional session.

Istanbul is literally where two continents meet, linked by the long bridges straddling the blue Bosphorus that divides the city. From Europe, and Engin Akin's living room, one can look out across the river and see Asia.

"Turkish food needs love" says Engin. A cookbook author and teacher, and general authority on Turkish cuisine, her place is my first port of call in Turkey for a cooking lesson. We sit and sip glasses of red tea and nibble on dried strawberries and chewy squares of *locum* - the real Turkish Delight - before getting down to business. This means my taking notes and trying not to get in the way too much as Engin and her assistants cook up a storm over the next few hours.

A feast of homestyle family dishes and regional specialities are prepared, explained, and set out on the large dining room table. *Manti*, the handmade Turkish ravioli, are poached in a tomato and chickpea broth and drizzled with two sauces: garlic yoghurt and a browned butter flavoured with dried mint. Plates hold lima beans, zucchini pancakes, a salad of purslane leaves, and crumbled fresh and aged sheep's cheese with Turkish olive oil. A cloud of aromatic steam unveils a rice pilaf studded with lamb shanks, raisins and almonds, spiced with a combination that includes *mastic*, made from the resin of a Mediterranean shrub.

Rice is also in the stuffing for chicken rubbed with red peppers and braised in a covered pot in the oven. *Borek* is a snaky coil of filo-like pastry, wound around a meat paste enlivened with dried currants and sweet spices like cinnamon. Best of all is a stew made of equal parts ground beef and lamb cooked up with onion, tomato, lots of eggplant peeled into zebra stripes and a fistful of whole garlic cloves.

. . . .

Being out and about the next day coincides with a huge rally taking place. Hundreds of thousands of Turks have taken to the streets, waving red flags in a demonstration over keeping religion and politics separate. The underground cisterns, harking back to Roman times, offer a cool respite from the bright bustle above. Nearby the cisterns is the Blue Mosque, built in the seventeenth century, the blue-tiled interior giving it its name. In a city whose skyline is filled with mosques, this may be the most impressive of them all.

At Topkapi Palace one tries to imagine the harem as it used to be, when concubines once lolled about watchful eunuchs (castrated African youths brought over to guard them). The blur of breathtaking ruins, dodgy bathrooms and terrible traffic continues. Istanbul's *taeksi* drivers can be pretty clueless and are some of the least knowledgeable I've ever encountered. Given the absence of training, directories or central assistance, it is hit and miss as to whether they have any idea where you are trying to get to.

. . . .

Engin's cooking has set a high benchmark which the first restaurateur does not reach. His internationally-lauded place serves up mushrooms straight out of a can at six US dollars a plate, with a bit of attitude for no extra charge. But after that experience, things rapidly improve. Develi's rooftop patio has one of the best views in the city out onto the Sea of Marmara, regarded contentedly by diners looking up from their olives, floppy flatbreads and assorted kebabs of skewered animal. *Dolma* refers to vegetables - zucchini, cabbage, vine leaves and peppers - stuffed with meat and rice. *Bulgur* is a pleasantly nutty tasting whole grain, perfect for absorbing the juices of a stew.

Ciga, on the Asian side of Istanbul, has an excellent *iskander kebap*, lamb shaved from a vertical skewer onto a plate with yoghurt sauce. The chef, Musa Dagdeviren, a tireless promoter of Turkish food, has visited the US several times to educate American cooks.

It takes a few attempts to find the hole-in-the-wall kebab place Seyhmuz, tucked into the warren of lanes surrounding the Grand Bazaar. The directions from the few vendors willing to help without a perusal of their wares first are confusing, until eventually a grizzled older gentleman points the way and nods gravely.

"Number One," he says.

Inside Seyhmuz a cook stands in front of a large pile of raw lamb meat with plenty of fat, working it back and forth with a two-handed cleaver to produce a finely-chopped mince. This is threaded onto skewers and grilled over coals before being folded into warm flatbread with flat leaf parsley, onion and tomato. It is, as my British friends would say, "the business".

Saturday evening in Istanbul and Engin rings to invite me out to a friend's apartment. Soon afterwards I find myself there playing Scrabble with three elegant Turkish ladies. The only native English speaker, I am beaten twice. And I was trying.

IMAM BAYILDI (BRAISED EGGPLANT)

Loosely inspired by my time in Engin Akin's kitchen. This would go well as part of a selection of vegetarian dishes, or as a side to roast lamb or grilled lamb chops. It may seem like quite a bit of garlic, but cooking the cloves whole makes them mellow and sweet.

Serves 4 as a side dish. Approximate cooking time: 1 hour 15 minutes, including brining the eggplant.

450 g (1 pound) eggplant (aubergines)
(about 2 small black/dark purple-skinned ones)

1 tablespoon plus ½ teaspoon salt, divided

450 g (1 pound) (about 4 medium) ripe-red tomatoes

90 ml (6 tablespoons) olive oil, divided, plus additional
for brushing the eggplant with

8 small cloves of garlic (about half a head of garlic)

4 tablespoons flat-leaf parsley, chopped

Freshly ground black pepper

1 tablespoon pine nuts, toasted in a dry pan until lightly browned
(careful - they burn quickly and it's invariably the moment
your back is turned)

Peel the eggplant lengthwise with a vegetable peeler, leaving a few strips of skin intact to create a striped effect ("like a zebra" as Engin would say). Cut the eggplant in half lengthways and then each piece in half crosswise. The main thing is to cut them into pieces about the same size so they cook evenly.

Dissolve 1 tablespoon of salt in a few tablespoons of water in a large bowl. Add the eggplant and enough water to cover, about 6 cups (1.5 litres), and weigh it down with a plate to keep submerged. Brine for 30 minutes, then remove from the water, squeeze gently and dry well with a paper towel until dry to the touch (the idea behind brining is to purge the eggplant of bitter juices and improve its texture - it doesn't make it salty).

Cut the tomatoes in half. Grate through the large holes of a box grater into a bowl and discard the skins.

Place a large, heavy-bottomed pot over medium-high heat. Add a tablespoon of oil and half of the eggplant slices, flat side down. Cook until nicely browned on the bottom, then brush the tops with more oil with a pastry brush or your fingers. Turn over and brown the other side well. Remove to a plate lined with paper towels and repeat with the remaining eggplant. (Cooking in two batches prevents crowding the pan and the slices steaming instead of browning.) Take your time with this step, and adjust the heat as needed to brown all the slices well but not blacken them.

Lower the heat to medium, add the remaining olive oil and the garlic and cook them until lightly golden but not brown. Place the eggplant back in the pot and pour the tomatoes over them. Add half of the parsley to the pot, the remaining ½ teaspoon of salt, a few generous grinds of black pepper and ½ cup (125 ml) water.

Cover and cook for 20 minutes, then uncover, turn the pieces over and cook another 10 minutes or so, uncovered, until the liquid has mostly evaporated and the eggplant has collapsed and is soft in a little bit of sauce ("eggplant in Turkey should be well done so it is creamy" says Engin).

Garnish with the remaining parsley and the pine nuts. Cool slightly and serve warm.

MOROCCO

The Dark Continent, they used to call it, for its unknown mysteries. My previous entry into Africa years ago was hurtling into a war zone in Somalia, burning with dengue fever, in a cargo plane full of ambulances and a vodka-swilling, chain-smoking crew of gold-teethed Russians. Which is another story.

This arrival is a more sedate one, and it is a first for me to be breakfasting in a garden where peacocks strut about the guests at the table. It's at Villa Mandarine in Rabat, a first stop after meeting up with a bunch of jetlagged Australians at Casablanca's Mohammed V Airport for a food tour of the country led by Aussie chef Christine Manfield. From Rabat we spend a few hours in a small bus, driving down through the historic city of Meknes for a picnic lunch in the Roman ruins of Volubilis (some of the ingredients for the lunch brought in from Australia). The ruins are in pretty good shape: some of the mosaics still with their original colours, storks nesting on the higher columns.

In Fes we plunge into the medieval era *medina* or old town; narrow, high-walled lanes only a few feet apart, lined with shops selling footwear, fabrics and food stuffs. Men wear long hooded robes while the women are clad in everything from jean and T-shirt combos to face-and-body-covering burkas. Plugged as the medina is with people, frequently there are shouts of warning and a donkey or motorbike squeezes through, leaving plenty of droppings underfoot (the donkey, that is).

At the meat shop every part of the animal is on sale, and as the customers haggle a butcher shaves tufts of hair from a severed cow's head with a straight-blade razor. Tannery workers toil away among pots of various dyes, flaying hides that have been softened with the acid from bird excrement. The smell is intense enough for passers-through to hold sprigs of mint under their nose as they look around.

··········

The walls and ramparts of Marrakech's 13th century medina are a pale pink, and it is flatter and wider than the steeper paths of Fes. Hotter, too. The *petit taxis* are red here. Morocco has two kinds of taxis: the long-distance ones that travel between towns and pick up passengers along the way, and the local version – *petit* – which are a different colour in each place (blue in Meknes, gold at Fes).

Sweet stores swarm with bees, but neither the shopkeepers nor customers seem to mind. In the main square snake charmers, water vendors and beggars compete for the attention of tourists. A morning spent inside the brightly-painted Spice Souk echoes with the patter of Arabic and French and dazzles the eye with coloured pyramids of spices, before leading into a visit to the old palace with its intricately-carved cedar ceilings.

I'm no great shakes as a bargainer but turn out to be better at it than one of the Australian girls, who at the end of the process hands over a higher sum than the original asking price. Outside the medina the city is quite Gallic in parts, with its pavement cafés and boulevards lined with trees.

Riads are Moroccan bed and breakfasts - old restored homes with rooms surrounding a courtyard, located inside or near the medina. Breakfast at the *riads* is always a lavish affair: yoghurt and fruit, crumpet-like pancakes called *beghir* and hard-boiled eggs with dipping saucers of salt and toasted cumin seed. The olives are some of the best I've tried, including a meaty purple kind rare outside the region.

To say there is a national sweet tooth is understating it - Moroccans rival Americans and the British in their love of all things sugar. A guide tells us that each person consumes an average of thirty kilograms (sixty-six pounds) of it per year. Honey, jams and marmalades are always on the breakfast table to spread on the various breads. Packets of sugar or sugar cubes for coffee drinkers are twice the regular size. Glasses of heavily-sweetened green tea with mint are served at all meals and throughout the day, *de rigeur* with any business transaction, poured from the pot in a high stream to froth up in the glass. Along with the mint tea may come a selection of sugary pastries too.

Spices common in the cooking are ginger, turmeric and coriander. The popular blend *ras-el-hanout* can contain as many as thirty spices, while cumin powder sits on the table as seasoning next to the salt and pepper. Despite the variety, the spices are often used in a muted and restrained way in the final mix, not making a statement in the way they do in, say, India. Their intent is to subtly augment the main item and bring out its flavour, rather than dominate it.

Besides parsley and fresh coriander leaves, other herbs don't seem to make a lot of appearances in the cooking. Mint is reserved for tea, and the great swaths of rosemary to be seen everywhere are not allowed anywhere near the lamb as they might be in other cuisines.

A pattern emerges to the Moroccan meal. It begins with an array of room temperature vegetable salads. Bowls of individually-prepared and spiced zucchini, cauliflower, eggplant, lentil, lima bean, peppers and cumin-scented batons of carrot are put out communally on the low tables for everyone to dip into. In a fancier place, such as La Maison Bleue back in Fes, might then be a *bstilla*, the famous pigeon pie (although often made with other poultry - we also see quail and chicken). *Bstilla* is made by manipulating layers of handkerchief-thin pastry (*warka*) to wrap up shredded meat and almonds, the pie finished with a sweet frosting of cinnamon sugar. This contrast of sweet and savoury, popular in Morocco today, was once standard in European cooking back in the Middle Ages.

After the *bstilla* is the *tagine*, a stew simmered over charcoal in a terracotta claypot with an open spout (the term *tagine* refers both to the finished dish and its vessel). Pieces of lamb, beef or chicken are combined with vegetables or fruit (dates, figs or prunes - that sweet tooth again) and nuts like walnuts or almonds. The meat is slowly cooked in its own juices, with a few spices and pungent flavour enhancers like olives and salty snips of preserved lemon. The fruit and vegetables are placed on top to steam rather than braise, retaining more of their integrity. In restaurants the contents are scooped out of the pot and portioned out at the table, and the flavoured liquid is always whisked back to the kitchens before I can grab a piece of bread to soak it up.

Couscous, tiny pasta laboriously hand rolled from semolina and flour, could follow. In a humbler restaurant it is served as a meal in its own right, emboldened by a few reluctant scraps of meat and the "seven vegetables" (carrot, turnip, parsnip, cabbage, zucchini, eggplant and pumpkin). No instant stuff here - the couscous takes hours to prepare, the grain sprinkled with water and formed into small pellets and cooked by steam over simmering broth. At la Maison Bleue it is finished with - have you guessed already? - a generous dusting of sugar.

···········

Saturday morning the *dada*, the female house cook at the *riad*, is making *msemen* for breakfast. She hand pats each one into shape - a sort of pancake folded over and over with minced green and black olives, zucchini and carrot. It fortifies me to roam around Marrakech's red streets and marketplaces until lunchtime at a street-front café just off one of the main drags.

The mixed grill starter does not hold enormous excitement in its little red sausages named *merguez*, dryish round *kefta* meatballs and skewers of slightly tough lamb. But then chicken, the house specialty, appears, prior to grilling quartered and coated with *chermoula*, a rustic paste of coriander, parsley, garlic, lemon juice and cumin. Apparently *chermoula* is ubiquitous around these parts, but its bursting flavour is new to me, and it instantly rockets into my mental list of top twenty-five foods (booting out, with little ceremony, the poor old Italian *pesto* that's been so good to me over the years).

I'm determined to try *khlea*, a preparation I have read of. Strips of beef are salted and sundried, and the jerky then simmered in beef tallow until tender and stored in the cooled fat like a Moroccan *confit*. I give one of the kids hanging around the entrance to the medina a few *dirhans* to show me to where the nearest *khlea* shop is. We are on the way when he stops to buy a candy bar at a sweet store with the money and is suddenly swooped on by a group of men, who shoo me away and start questioning him. "He was taken to the police station," a vendor informs me later.

Alone now, I finally find the man selling *khlea* and also *agrisse*, the debris left after making it. The suggestion is that it's best sautéed crisp with eggs for breakfast, but that's not an option here. I settle for spooning a few grams cold out of a plastic bag. It tastes like the contents of that can of roast drippings your grandmother might have kept under the sink in the kitchen.

· · · · · · · · · ·

To reach the Kasbah du Toubkal it is first necessary to trek a few hours by bus from Marrakech into the foothills of the High Atlas Mountains, passing through hard rocky ground stubbled with green bushes. Goats thread their way along the hillside as the path narrows and inclines. The village of Imlil is as far as the road can go, and the final ascent is by mule up a steep wind to the Kasbah.

From the rooftop of the Kasbah by day the view stretches for miles in every direction, deep valleys and mountain ranges dotted sparely with distant villages. Looming above is the snow-capped peak of Ibel Toubkal, the highest mountain in North Africa. Night is equally stunning, the clear sky overhead a sparkling ceiling of stars. Morning means soothing sounds of birdsong and rushing water from the waterfall-fed stream below - but also the nearby rooster and the 4.30 am call to prayer.

The area is home to the Berber tribe, the original nomadic inhabitants, and the Kasbah is run with a view to sustainability by a British company in partnership with the local Berber community. In the surrounding villages the way of life has changed little for centuries, electricity coming to this remote spot only ten years ago, the telephone a couple of years later.

The more energetic of us have the opportunity to do some hiking. The first time we set out we get lost and eventually make our way back to the Kasbah by following the path of the river, slipping and sliding down the slopes and dislodging rocks that go crashing down through the undergrowth. The next day, with a local guide this time, it is a climb of several hours to the Tizi N'Tichka pass for views both of the valley we have just come up from and down into the Imara Valley on the other side. We celebrate at the top with mint tea before beginning the (much easier) trip down.

Tuesday afternoon is given over to the making of *mechoui*. This traditional feast begins with the staff lighting a fire inside a giant, jar-shaped clay pot in the garden, similar to an Indian tandoor oven but much larger. When after a few hours the flames have died down, the Berber in charge dipping his arm in to gauge the temperature, it is judged ready.

A whole, unseasoned sheep torso, speared through with a wooden branch, is rinsed with water and lowered vertically into the oven. The lid is replaced and completely sealed with mud, and the *mechoui* left undisturbed for several hours until done, lifted out by torchlight and transferred to the kitchen to be hacked up. We tear off pieces of the flesh, pressing them into bowls of salt and ground cumin or the fiery condiment called *harissa*.

. . . .

Under the shade of fig trees in the garden grounds of La Maison Arabe, back in Marrakech, cooking school is in session. We embark on making seafood *bstilla* under the guidance of the *dada* by making a filling of diced fish and squid with small prawns. This mixture is cooked, combined with vermicelli noodles and allowed to cool. We trim *warka* pastry into circles, wrap a couple of layers around our seafood and fry up the bstilla in oil. As we eat in the garden, near where the herbs for the kitchen are grown, I'm pretty self-impressed with mine. Until, that is, I look around at the plates of my fellow novices and see their efforts are all much more photogenic.

One cannot leave Morocco without mention of *smen*, one of the major fats used in the cooking and essentially rancid butter. Moroccans have developed a taste for it, but I have not. It can be approximated at home by mixing a little strong blue cheese into softened butter.

CHERMOULA (Moroccan marinade)

This marinade makes enough for two quartered medium chickens or an equivalent quantity of chicken pieces. Or use it as a marinade for other meats such as lamb, or to marinate fish for up to an hour before cooking.

Serves 8 as part of a barbecue lunch. Prepare ahead: Marinate chicken 2 hours up to overnight.

One bunch each fresh coriander (cilantro) and flat-leaf parsley

4 garlic cloves, roughly chopped

3 tablespoons (45 ml) freshly squeezed lemon juice (about 1 lemon)

1 tablespoon (15 ml) red or white wine vinegar

2½ teaspoons ground cumin

3½ teaspoons ground coriander

1 tablespoon sweet paprika, preferably Hungarian

½ teaspoon cayenne or 1 teaspoon red chilli flakes

1 teaspoon freshly ground black pepper

2 teaspoons grated ginger (optional)

Salt

¼-½ cup (60 ml – 125 ml) extra virgin olive oil, or as needed

2 quartered medium chickens (about 1.5 kg or 3 pounds each),
or an equivalent quantity of chicken pieces

Purée all the ingredients except the chicken in a blender, adding more olive oil as needed to make a thick paste. Add salt – it should taste quite salty by itself as it is a condiment.

Reserve a third of the marinade. Place the chicken pieces in a large bowl and rub the rest of the marinade into the chicken. Cover and marinate in the refrigerator for 2 hours, up to overnight.

Grill the chicken slowly, or roast in a moderate oven, until the juices run clear yellow, not pink, when pierced with a fork. Brush reserved marinade over the chicken while cooking.

PART THREE
NORTH AMERICA

MEXICO

....,...................

Mexico can come as something of a culinary shock. Visitors arriving from around the world, bringing with them preconceptions of what they think of as Mexican food, may find they are hardly realized. No dairy-and-fat-heavy Tex-Mex here; no crunchy taco shells or rice-stuffed burritos snug enough under their blanket of melted cheese.

All that can be great stuff! But here the flavours are more charred - burnt even, not as smoothed out, bordering on bitter. Leaner and a little bit meaner. A great deal of blackening of ingredients goes on; tomatoes, peppers, onions and garlic all blistered over flames or under the broiler before going into the *molcajete* (mortar) to be pounded into sauces and pastes (or, more prosaically these days, into a blender).

The importance of corn: softened in an alkaline solution, it is ground into *masa*, a dough used to make the numerous *antojitos* – snacks - eaten throughout the day. *Tortillas*, masa pancakes, are filled to make tacos, sauced to make enchiladas, fried flat as tostadas or made into chips. Leftovers of those chips, re-doused in sauce and baked, create the comfort food *chilaquiles*. Combine masa with some meat or fat, sheath in a corn husk and steam and you have *tamales*. Dried kernels of the corn are cooked into a nourishing soup named *posole*, a long-simmered broth that is freshened with sliced avocado and brightened with *cilantro* (fresh coriander leaf) and wedges of lime.

The importance of chillies: they are the real essence of the cuisine. Dozens of varieties are used - fresh, dried, or canned, utilised alone or in combinations by the cook like an artist mixing colours. The spectrum is enormous - nutty *cascabel*, searing *arbol*, the bright heat of *piquin*, the punch of *habaneros*, the milder and more utilitarian *ancho* and *mulato*. The same chilli pepper may vary in name if it is fresh or dried and from state to state in Mexico, adding to the confusion of the uninitiated.

The basic technique of using dried chillies is to de-seed, toast and rehydrate them in hot water, meanwhile roasting onion and garlic. Purée everything together, season and strain if desired, and this is salsa. Or heat to reduce and caramelize, thin with broth to a consistency of heavy cream, and the makings of a soup or stew is underway.

The importance of beans: eaten together with corn, they form a complete protein and were the staple diet of the Indians prior to Spanish invasion. Black and the pinkish pinto are the commonly seen types of bean, cooked "a la olla" (in the pot) with herbs and a bit of fresh or cured pork if at hand to make a low cost, filling meal.

··········

In Saltillo in northern Mexico I catch up with my friend Lilia. Decades ago her parents opened a taco stand specialising in *cabrito*, kid goat, a delicacy of the region. The business, now run by their children, including Lily, has grown to include several casual eateries, a fine dining restaurant and a large banquet and catering service. The Cardenas have become a major economic force of the town. In addition to generations of hungry Saltillo residents, they have fed visiting celebrities and several presidents.

In 48 hours Lily and her family whisk me to nine places ranging from *taquerias* to sit-down restaurants. I'm never allowed to open my wallet, and at the hotel they have put me up in the bill mysteriously disappears. Lily's brother Eduardo takes us out to their abattoir, a slaughterhouse set in the fields near Saltillo. Here I get to see the whole, sobering process from gambolling kid to hanging carcass of meat – a process that takes mere minutes.

Back at their busy Meson Principal restaurant *cabrito* is the main event, the goats skewered whole through the spine and simply roasted without even salt, a taste for the purist that is enlivened tableside with the fiendishly good house salsa (I plead for the recipe, and get it, but am not sure if I am allowed to share with you the secret ingredient).

· · · · · · · · · ·

At a bank machine in Mexico City I draw a decent sum of money out, but a day later have almost nothing left. I can only assume I've handed over 1000 pesos somewhere and not 100, the equivalent of paying US $100 instead of $10. Somebody's day - or month - has been made.

Ciudad de Mexico is the largest city in the world, so it is fitting that it has the world's largest food market. The Merced takes up two full city blocks, housing over three thousand stalls with the adjacent buildings selling still more stuff. I have never seen many of the vegetables and fruits before and would have no idea how to prepare them. Unlike the Mexican chillies imported to other countries, hard and desiccated in their plastic sleeves, the ones here at the market remind you that really they are dried fruit, pliable and soft and aromatic.

In the food court customers are eating *huaraches*, another *antojito*, the masa dough formed into boats and splashed with salsa and crumbles of fresh cheese. I keep an eye out for pickpockets in the busy market, but as I've already made that thousand-peso mistake it will be slim pickings for them if they do get to me.

· · · · · · · · · ·

Rick Bayless gives a talk in Mexico City. The best known Mexican restaurateur in the US (Oklahoma born and bred) discusses why Mexican cuisine is much more diverse than is generally known north of the border. It is a tale of conquerors and immigrants. The native Indians had an indigenous cuisine of beans, corn, chocolate and chilli peppers. In the sixteenth century the invading Spanish brought with them bread, the pig, sugar and spices.

Influences from Arab cooking also came with the Spaniards - at the time Spain considered more part of the Arab world than Europe. It explains a link I've been curious about between India and Mexico. The two countries have a common palette of unleavened breads, dried legumes and chillies and a love of the herb *cilantro*. The spices in Arab cuisine like cumin and coriander which are commonly used in India also found their way to Mexico.

But despite starting out with many of the same ingredients, very different results are yielded. In Mexico they want to taste the chillies - spices are "actors in the background", to quote chef Roberto Santibanez. India, on the other hand, may grow a variety of chillies but they seem to be used primarily for their qualities of heat and colour. It's their turn there to be the supporting cast to spice.

During his presentation Bayless takes his small audience on a culinary tour of Mexico, starting at the US border with the origins of "Tex-Mex". The northern desert, where Lily lives, is bread, flour tortillas instead of corn, beef and goat; simple flavours. The Veracruz area is famous for its seafood preparations, while the Yucatan, down on the Caribbean side, is ethnically different – Mayan, not Aztec – and what they eat more resembles Guatemalan food. Central Mexico, where we are now, is the most sophisticated, drawing on imperial and European influences and more modern ideas. The *al pastor* taco stands everywhere in Mexico City are one fairly modern innovation, adapted from a tradition of Lebanese migrants - pork replacing lamb on the vertical spit and *tortillas* filling in for Lebanese flatbread.

Pujol represents an example of culinary modernism in Mexico City, a small restaurant which is starting to earn big praise on an international scale. I dine there on my last night in the city. Even though it is very enjoyable, as I eat I sense I am missing a whole layer of reference. The refined meal may be ultra-contemporary and global-looking with its foams and temperature specific cooking techniques, but there are glimpses that it is quoting and riffing on traditional local preparations. I am only dimly aware of these, but this would really resonate with someone who has grown up with the originals.

· · · · · · · · · ·

I keep eyeing the hot dog vendors in the constitution square of the colonial city of Tlaxcala. The griddled hot dogs, wrapped in bacon and squirted with an array of condiments, do look - and smell - good. But at what cost to the intestinal system to eat one? After several days of dithering, I finally take the plunge, and am fine. A friend, inspired, follows my lead – and is not.

Tlaxcala is a major *pulque* producer of Mexico, *pulque* being a fermented sweet liquid from the maguey plant (from which mescal and tequila are also derived). I visit a *pulque* hacienda to see it being made - it doesn't look a terribly hygienic method. Luckily they strain out the dead flies before bottling. The musty taste of pulque is one that is... acquired, I think.

· · · · · · · · · ·

With only two days in Oaxaca it's necessary to hit the ground running, and over a weekend I sample five of the city's famed seven *moles*.

Mole, ('moh-lay') translates as sauce (so *guacamole* – avocado sauce) but the *moles* of Oaxaca are more like complex stews, containing up to thirty ingredients and thickened with bread, seeds and nuts. Moving from street to street and restaurant to restaurant I try in turn *verde, negro, rojo, amarillo* and *coloradito.*

By now a certain culinary fatigue has set in. A restaurateur at a place overlooking the main square senses this and talks me into a reviving shot of artisanal tequila. It's a far cry (or sip) from the bathtub stuff I first tried years ago in Tijuana. Thus restored, I find I may have some stomach room if I can locate any establishments serving the remaining two *moles (chichilo* and *manchamantel* - "tablecloth stainer").*

Then disaster strikes. Who knows what did it? Was it the unpasteurised rose petal ice cream? The crisp, spicy *chapulines* - grasshoppers - that I initially mistook for shredded beef jerky? The street snack of tacos filled with slippery stewed pig skin and green chilli? Or did one of the *moles* exact Montezuma's Revenge?

My chief suspicion is that it was earlier in the afternoon at the market. Faced with a bustling food vendor filled to capacity, and one standing forlornly alongside with empty seats, I ignored all advice on what you are supposed to do in this situation and chose the latter. In any case, whatever the cause, I have severe food poisoning.

One of the longest days of my life follows: by bus to Oaxaca's airport, flying north in a semi-conscious state to Mexico City, an interminable wait around in the terminal there for a few hours, another flight to Los Angeles, a transit there for several hours more, delirious, dehydrated and nauseous, before finally boarding my plane to Canada. Mexican food, I still love you, but you can have a sting in your tail.

GUACAMOLE (AVOCADO DIP)

Serve with tortilla chips for dunking. It's also good as condiment for Icelandic graflax (p 141) or the Spanish beans (p 118) .

If the avocados are unripe and still too firm when you buy them, the trick, apparently, is to store them in a paper bag with a banana, which speeds the ripening process. Should they stubbornly refuse to do so, a trick from my friend Erna is to dice them very finely, instead of mashing, and then combine with the other ingredients.

Serves 4 as a snack or appetiser.

½ small white or red onion, very finely chopped

2-3 tablespoons chopped fresh coriander leaf
(cilantro), including stems

3 ripe avocados, preferably Haas

Scant ½ teaspoon salt

Juice of half a lime or lemon

1 small tomato, skinned, de-seeded and diced (optional)

1-2 jalapeno chillies, de-seeded and diced (optional)

Combine onion and coriander in a medium bowl. Halve the avocados and remove the pits. Scoop out the flesh, add to the onion mixture and mash coarsely. Stir in the salt and lime juice, and the tomato and chilli if using.

Taste and add more lime juice and salt if needed. The idea is to use enough salt and lime to coax out the flavor of the avocado, but not overpower it. If not serving the guacamole immediately, cover with plastic wrap (cling film) pressed directly onto the surface of the guacamole to prevent oxidation.

CANADA

In the province of British Columbia, nestled between the water and mountains, Vancouver has as beautiful a setting as any city in the world. The green expanse of Stanley Park runs to one side and sunsets streak the sky over English Bay purple and orange. Grouse Mountain rises up to the north – at night the lights of its ski-run like a spaceship floating above the city.

Bring a weatherproof jacket – the rainy season runs from July to June. Despite this, Vancouverites are an outdoorsy lot, spurning umbrellas while rollerblading to work and heading out on their weekends to ski or snowboard nearby Whistler in winter and hike it in the summer. Kayakers paddle along English Bay between the boats, as seaplanes take off from Canada Bay bound for Vancouver Island and the town of Victoria with its British-styled tearooms and pubs.

Canadians are considerate to a fault, removing their shoes when entering a home and calling out 'thank you' to the driver when they depart a public bus, and this politeness extends to the Vancouver traffic. If you step out onto the middle of a busy street, the cars will – usually! - slow for you, with nary a driver honking an irate horn at the jaywalking pedestrian. I wonder how many Canadians casually do this in Saigon or the Big Apple and get flattened. (It may be mostly a West Coast Thing - across the other side of the country in Toronto road relations are not nearly so sedate.)

Vancouver has more of the feeling of a big town than a city. The downtown is small – just several cross streets really – and if you spend any amount of time here you will start running into people you know. Or think you know, but realize it's a famous face or two – Vancouver is known as "Hollywood North" for the volume of film and TV productions it hosts. The crews and trailers take up many of the side streets and alleyways. For locals it's not unusual to be watching a Hollywood blockbuster set somewhere in the US and think "Manhattan? That's Robson Street, near Burrard!" Willing suspension of disbelief is necessary for the moviegoer who knows this place.

Granville Island is the shopping mecca for fresh produce and tourist trinkets. Under the Granville Bridge, it's accessed by foot or car on the south side, or a two-minute ferry ride across English Bay from the West End. It showcases Edenic ingredients, sides of BC salmon and Alberta beef, fiddleheads for a brief few weeks in the spring and summer strawberries that are as intense as I've tasted.

So far it all sounds picturesque, but a darker side lurks in the blighted intersection of Main and Hastings a few blocks from downtown's core. This is ground zero for drug addicts and the homeless. Here meth, heroin and crack are dealt and taken openly. Among needle-exchange shelters and raddled streetwalkers are some of the most down and out of North America, decimated by poverty and narcotics, living their lives on the street. The displaced and the disturbed across the country drift west to the more temperate climates of British Columbia. One friend of mine a few years ago succumbed here to the lure of crack and was swallowed up into the streets around Main. Another friend got caught up with drugs too, a life ending far too young in still murky circumstances.

The Chinese takeover of Hong Kong in 1997 sparked a major emigration of Chinese to Vancouver (including a number of notable chefs). A Chinatown sits next to Main & Hastings, but as in many other cities of the world, the real action is out in the suburbs – in this case Richmond, towards the airport. It's all here – the malls filled with early morning tai chi practitioners, supermarkets filled with fascinating groceries, giant dim sum palaces packed to capacity on weekends.

. . . .

Canada's main claims to culinary fame come from the east, the French-speaking and influenced province of Quebec. I think it's reasonable to say that traditionally, much of the rest of the country wasn't as food oriented. For many people meals were fuel, a necessary interruption to the true purpose of each day. It just wasn't something to think about all that much. As that changes a movement is emerging, as elsewhere in the world, to embrace the local and seasonal. It goes by many names, and usually indicates ingredients of a region prepared and cooked with French technique. Here in Vancouver it is known as Pacific Northwestern cuisine, and features in the more upmarket restaurants.

On the other hand, despite the natural bounty available, the population still has a deep fondness for processed food like Jell-O, an artificially-flavoured gelatin dessert, and KD – Kraft Dinner, packaged macaroni and cheese with a powdered sauce which, once reconstituted, is a fluorescent orange. Tim Hortons is a beloved coffee and doughnuts chain. Canadians, who apparently eat more doughnuts per head than even Americans, won't hear a word said against it, and no event's complete without someone turning up with a box of the doughnut holes called Timbits. Unfortunately, and with apologies to my Canadian friends, Timbits, to me, just aren't very good. The company's slogan is "Always Fresh" but, once it was reported that the doughnuts are par-cooked in a midwest facility, flash frozen and shipped out to outlets around the country, a friend dubbed them "Almost Fresh".

Ordering a Caesar in the rest of North America will get you a salad with a creamy dressing in which anchovies may figure, but in this corner of the world it means the local competitor to the Bloody Mary – a glass of vodka with "clamato", clam and tomato juice.

For the real Canadian comfort cooking it's largely those imports from Quebec. Hearty stuff for lumberjacks – from split pea soup to sugar pie and maple syrup. Jewish food out of Quebec's Montreal means properly boiled-then-baked bagels and smoked meat, a corned beef cut smoked and spiced somewhat like pastrami. (The best smoked meat sandwiches in Vancouver, though tasty, can't rival those of smoked meat sanctuaries like Schwartz's Deli in Montreal.)

Poutine is a Quebecois mess of French fries drowned in beef gravy and topped with fresh cheese curds. The gravy seeps into the fries, making them limp and wet, and the cheese barely melts and stays in lumps that squeak between the teeth. It's delicious.

It's even available in Vancouver in the fast food chains like Burger King and KFC, although their versions don't do it justice.

"The gravy is completely vegetarian," says the server.

"Really! So what's in it?"

"It's... um... It's... I think... let me check with the manager".

No one, on this particular day, can supply an answer.

GELEE DE VIN
(WINE AND FRUIT GELATIN DESSERT)

An adult take on the Jell-O beloved by generations of Canadian children. And very pretty too, with the fruits suspended in it. I have given it the Quebecois-sounding French name just because "Gelée de Vin" sounds better than "Wine Gelatin", doesn't it? The fashion currently in restaurants is to serve a very loose jelly, barely set, but I like a firmer version.

Gelatin's strength and directions for use can vary from country to country, so check the packet to confirm how much to use and how to add it. (I haven't always heeded my own advice, and have ended up with either a soup that never sets or a bowl of clear rubber you could bounce a coin off.)

To use strawberries in this reminds me of the time I was blown away by the incredible local berries I tasted at Granville Island Public Market in Vancouver (and the wine reminds me of the fine British Columbia wines that market offers too), but you can choose any combination of fruits you want. Do beware of certain fruits like pineapple and kiwi, which contain enzymes that interfere with gelatin setting.

Regarding which wine to choose, I subscribe to the maxim of always using a wine in recipes that you would be happy to drink - no 'cooking wine' or leftovers that have been lurking in the fridge

Serves 4. Preparation time: A minimum of 6 hours including setting time, preferably longer to ensure setting. (Making it the night before should ensure it sets thoroughly.)

3 or more gelatin sheets (leaves), (check packet for guideline to quantity) preferably platinum or gold grade, or 1 tablespoon unflavoured powdered gelatin

1½ cups (375 ml) wine, such as champagne, rose or pinot noir

½ cup (100 g) caster sugar

100-150 g (3½-5 ounces) assorted fruit, such as strawberries & sliced banana, or raspberries and sliced peaches, or pitted cherries or mixed different coloured berries.

Soak the gelatin sheets in cold water to soften. In a small saucepan on low heat, stir wine and sugar gently until the sugar is dissolved. Remove from the heat. Remove the gelatin sheets from the water, squeeze excess water out of them and stir into the wine until dissolved. (If using powdered gelatin instead, sprinkle it over ¼ cup (60 ml) of the wine and let stand 5 minutes. Heat the remaining wine with the sugar, then stir in the gelatin mixture until dissolved and let cool.) Skim off and discard any froth.

Pour 2 tablespoons (30 ml) of the liquid into each of four glasses and divide the fruit among each glass. Chill in the refrigerator until just starting to set, then add the rest of the liquid and return to the refrigerator for at least 6 hours (preferably longer) to set.

USA

HAWAII

Palm trees and high-rise apartments. Bronzed surfers and barely-bikinied beach babes beneath low hanging clouds that brush against the mountain tops. Waikiki on the island of Oahu is my base for a few days as I plan an assault on the US mainland, where I'll be renting a car for what will - hopefully - be an epic road trip from coast to coast.

Travelling around the world with just a carry-on bag means paring clothing down to the absolute essentials. A couple of long sleeved shirts, a pair of dark pants and a pair of black leather shoes. All-purpose wear designed to fit in with a range of situations, from being out and about sightseeing to sitting down at a diner or a fine dining restaurant. In most places, dressing this way is the most likely way to blend in, to some extent, with the locals. Here, amongst all the aloha shirts and permatans? Not so much. Time to go for lunch.

Hawaiian food fuses elements from American, Japanese, Korean, Filipino, Portuguese and Pacific island cooking, a collision of cultures with unique results. 7-Eleven convenience stores sell *musubi*, like a sushi hand roll but with the centre of raw fish replaced by a slice of Spam. Yes, Spam, that ultra-processed tinned luncheon product, butt of so many jokes but here, before being inserted between the rice and seaweed, pan-glazed in teriyaki sauce to become crisp and meaty. Not so Spam-ish now, more reminiscent of the lacquered squares of barbecued pork found in Singapore and Malaysia. (Spam remains very popular in parts of the world. Back in the Philippines a supermarket had most of one aisle dedicated to it.) Red-skinned hot dog *musubi* are an alternative, a bargain meal at a dollar each.

The plate lunch is another Hawaiian institution - two scoops of white rice and one of gluey macaroni salad with a choice of various proteins. Portions everywhere, by the way, are huge. *Loco Moco* is a hamburger patty and two fried eggs over a mound of rice, all awash in brown gravy. The seafood salad *poke* is a bit more restrained – dark crimson dice of ahi tuna or other fish tossed with soy sauce, green onion, chilli pepper and sesame oil (sometimes too much sesame oil: a little of that stuff goes a long way). In a "*Poke* Bowl" the chilled fish sits atop warm rice for a nice contrast in temperatures. *Lomi lomi*, a cold salmon dish where the fish is hacked into pieces with a sharp knife, is also the description of a local type of massage. Best not to confuse the two.

Alan Wong's Pineapple Room, a sort-of-upscale place inside a department store, has the island food of smoky *kalua* pig plus *poi*, a paste made of pounded taro root. At a local dive called Ono, *lualua* is a combination of pork and salted butterfish steamed in taro leaves. Down the street from Ono a stand sells rainbow *shave ice*, cones of powdered ice streaked with garish hues of brightly coloured syrups. It's refreshing, though there's nothing natural in those syrup bottles.

Fifty years ago Leonard Rego, grandson of Portuguese immigrants, opened a small bakery with his mother's *malasada* recipe on the menu. The holeless, slightly underdone doughnuts are now a quintessential part of the Honolulu experience. Leonard's cooks up a batch every few minutes so they are warm and fresh. These pillowy perfections have also jumped ship to nearby bakery Champion's (a defector from Leonard's). They have grown up a bit there, and are sourer and yeastier.

Not far away at Mavro, the *malasadas* are reincarnated as little balls of deep-fried brioche with a liquid centre of passion fruit curd. Nestled on a puddle of guava purée against a scoop of pineapple ice cream, they are softer and eggier than Leonard's, closer in nature to the *beignets* of the chef's native France.

More *malasadas* are available around the island: square ones, ones with holes, others plumped full of coconut into little balloons of bliss. In the name of research I try as many as I can.

ROAD TRIP – USA COAST TO COAST
CALIFORNIA

All big cities have a "no go" or at least "be cautious" zone, but in San Francisco the atmosphere can change by the street instead of the neighbourhood. Go a block from bustling Union Square's hotels and major brand stores and immediately it is barred up shops and adult emporiums, the addicted and homeless shuffling along the sidewalks. Walk a street or two further and the scene has already changed again, giving way to young urban couples, boutique coffee houses and ethnic grocers.

San Francisco's famous hills add a touch of cardio to the walking, turning it into exercise. Cable cars and street cars glide up and down the steep inclines. Mornings and evenings have a chill to them but the days warm rapidly, and by midday the sun is heating the pavement.

Sitting at the counter at Boulevard restaurant near the ferry terminal, I'm in awe at the speed of the line cooks working away inches from me. Under pressure they turn out dish after consistent dish, although they'd clearly be happy with a few more seconds with each plate. Multi-tasking, the cooks spoon foaming butter over pan-roasted meats and manipulate squeeze bottles, constantly whirling to transfer items of different degrees of doneness in and out of or between ovens and grills. It's the theatre of watching skilled pianists playing different parts with each hand while working the pedals with their feet, with the added benefit of getting to eat the creations.

My friend Sabrina - whose tiny frame belies her healthy appetite - has arrived just in time for dinner. We go to Michael Mina, a gloomily-lit restaurant in the Westin St Francis hotel. The menu is based on the "trio" concept, a main ingredient – lamb chop, for instance, or fillet of sole - presented three different ways on specially striated plates with three different sauces: "Curry, Black Olive, Heirloom Tomato".

A cable car ride away through some of the priciest real estate in the US is Gary Danko's at the edge of Fisherman's Wharf. From the list of desserts, out jumps "Blueberry French Toast with Maple Syrup Emulsion and Salted Almond Ice Cream". The bread-pudding-like French toast has been made of croissant, all the better to soak up its custard bath before frying. Afterwards at the Wharf, Sabrina buys me a glass snail, possibly as a hint after how quickly she's just seen me inhale dessert.

We spend a day up in the wine country of nearby Napa, and then head south. On Highway One the green hills of northern California are swaddled in mist and fog, on the coastline below water foaming about the rocks and gulls skimming across white-tipped waves. Around Big Sur the road seems to curl out above the clouds that cling close to the sea below. During the twelve-hour drive (with stops) along the coast a more southern Californian roadside begins to emerge, gradually, of palm trees and sand beaches.

Soon the hills have all gone, replaced by flat streets, strip malls and more palms - it must be Los Angeles. The City of Angels, where your taxi driver or restaurant server is as likely as not an aspiring actor or scriptwriter. At the first place we lunch a man at the next table is busy pitching his movie idea to a couple of bored-looking producers. Afterwards I drop Sabrina off, her role on this road trip only a cameo – as a working actor LA is her home town.

The free local weekly magazine has nine advertisements in the first fifteen pages for plastic surgery ("Spring Special: $1000 Off Breast Augmentation/Reduction") and cosmetic dentistry ("One Hour Smile Makeover"), as well as plugs for chin and cheek implants ("Natural Looking Results, Not Overdone!") and liposuction ("Lunchtime Special: Remove Unwanted Fat In 2 Hours"). There are not only facial ("One Hour

Face Lift $3900") but brow and neck lifts too, plus any other area that you might care to have touched up ("Vaginal Rejuvenation: $2500").

The night soundtrack of sirens and helicopters with spotlights whirring overhead reminds the visitor it's not the safest of cities. It's a slight relief to see the back of a couple of neighbourhoods, although they've been worth the visit for their food. Waiting in line at a taco truck in East LA, I'm approached by a group of young Latino men, not with bad intentions but a puzzled "Why are you here?"

At Pizzeria Mozza, newly opened at the corner of Highland and Melrose in Hollywood, a queue of people is waiting to grab seats at the non-reservation bar once it opens. I take my place at the back, and am outraged a few minutes later when some newcomers head straight to the other end. They avoid my glare, although other people keep glancing at me. Then the doors swing wide for business - right behind me. The awful truth is revealed - I am the one who has crashed the front of the line. No one has said anything, perhaps as I have been glowering angrily at them all. Having a seat now at the bar straight away does seem to be tempering my guilt.

The pizza at Mozza is better than at many places in Italy. Pencil-thin asparagus spears, crunchy wisps of pancetta and cream-centred burrata cheese top the crust with its puffy edged rim. The owners of Mozza are not Italian but American Italophiles - as fervent in their zeal as any born-again religionist.

LA has such huge immigrant populations that the food can be every way as authentic as in the countries of origin. It houses the biggest number of Koreans in a city other than Seoul, of Vietnamese outside of Indochina, of Armenians ex Armenia. The Fairfax district's Little Ethiopia offers spaghetti accented with African spices. On nearby Venice Boulevard one can sit down to a true Brazilian *feijoada*, black beans stewed with a multitude of unmentionable piggy bits and garnished correctly with toasted *manioc* flour.

Mexican and Latin American food remain the most ubiquitous here with the proximity to the border. You can have your pick of specific regions of Mexico or choose Californian Mexican, "Cal-Mex". A "wet" burrito, at Diana's on Sepulveda, is pure Cal-Mex comfort food - a whole meal's worth of braised beef, rice and beans wrapped up in a floppy flour tortilla, steamed and submerged in chilli sauce and melted cheese. It's hard to restrain an involuntary moan of pleasure at the first bite.

Outside of Hawaii, a hot doughnut remains really hard to find in North America except for the Krispy Kreme chain. I get up one morning at 4 am and drive to two famous places, hoping to catch the bakers at work and plead for one straight out of the fryer. At Stan's Donuts in Westwood, no luck. At Bob's at the Farmers Market on Fairfax I have to settle for lukewarm.

The next day it's a 5.30 am start for the thirty-five-mile drive to outer Glendora to Donut Man - but again in vain. The doughnuts were made at 2 am. Some consolation is that Donut Man make their fillings with seasonal fruit from nearby farms. Today it is peaches.

NEVADA

Out in the desert, in the middle of nowhere, suddenly up loom the huge facades of the hotel-casinos. There rises the New York skyline, behind it a scale replica of the Eiffel Tower. A giant pyramid and sphinx sit next to a Disneyfied medieval castle, beyond that a Venetian fantasy complete with gondolas and canals.

At a hotel lobby early one morning it might as well be Saturday night – the ground floor casino is filled with people drinking heavily and gambling, gathered around card tables or forcing coins into slot machines. Twenty-four hours of every day visitors flock in to "Lost Wages" to hit the casinos or party until the small hours (or the following morning, or the following afternoon) at the bars and nightclubs congregated along the main strip.

Of all its reputations, the one Las Vegas didn't always have was for good food. It was more about all-you-can-eat buffets and cheap steakhouse dinners. While that'll always stay a part of the scene, Vegas has evolved into one of the major restaurant destinations in the world. Wolfgang Puck kick-started it all some fifteen years ago by opening an outpost of his LA restaurant, Spago.

Other name chefs followed suit, and with the floodgates thrown wide, famed, acclaimed restaurants from New York to Boston to Chicago, San Francisco to Santa Fe are now all represented here. International stars are getting in on the act too. Multi-Michelin starred French chefs such as Joël Robuchon, voted "Chef of the 20th Century" by his peers, Guy Savoy and Alain Ducasse have recently landed. (The seventeen course menu of carefully constructed flavours at Robuchon's the year before was the greatest restaurant experience I have had - and also by far the most expensive.)

Critics say it's all for show, and that the casinos are spending large sums for the big names to draw in the punters while the actual superstar chefs themselves are hardly ever on the premises. Today's *Las Vegas Review-Journal* addresses the issue: "An absentee chef arrangement can be an iffy proposition - successful if the star in question manages to put the right chef de cuisine in place and give him (or her) his head, but not if he's a control freak or really bad at hiring."

Recently, one celebrity chef and empire builder responded when asked who cooks the food in his kitchens when he's not in: "The same person who cooks it when I *am* there!" Although it's nice to fantasize that the person whose name is above the door is lurking just behind the pass, anxiously gauging your reaction to the meal, it doesn't matter too much to me, as long as the food is good.

California-based Michael Mina has eight restaurants around the US, including four in Vegas. He can't be everywhere at once. His San Francisco flagship was outstanding, so it's an opportunity to see in Vegas what happens when the marquee name has – temporarily, at least - left the building. At Nobhill in the MGM Grand, highlights are a satay stick appetiser of flatiron steak poached in butter and soy, and moist pancetta-wrapped Kurobuta pork with red lentils and mustard. But the "molten" chocolate cupcake... isn't. It's overbaked so the centre is bone dry, negating the point of the dish. The server then tries to claim that's how it's supposed to be.

At Mina's new steakhouse at Mandalay Bay, Stripsteak, the menu is innovative and enticing but the execution of every item I order is disappointing: the French fries cold, the steak oversalted, the pastries clumsy. The overall impression is that, like mere mortals, even brilliant chefs can see consistency suffer as they expand their brand.

· · · · · · · · · ·

Vegas is synonymous with excess, so it feels right that Fleur De Lys at Mandalay Bay has a five-thousand-dollar hamburger. A few years back a chef in New York put a Twenty-seven-dollar foie-gras-and-truffle-stuffed burger on his menu, sparking headlines. Those were the innocent days when Twenty-seven dollars seemed outrageous for a burger. A burger war broke out as a nearby restaurant came up with a forty-nine-dollar Kobe beef burger. The original chef responded by doubling the number of truffles and hiking his price tag to fifty-nine dollars. And so on it went. When the smoke cleared he was still on top, with a price tag of ninety-nine dollars and even more truffle packed between the buns.

That burger's available in Vegas by now of course, at – naturally - the cloned outpost of the original restaurant. Meanwhile the Fleur De Lys five-thousand-dollar burger has its share of foie gras, truffles and Kobe beef, and includes a side of high grade caviar and a bottle of fancy champagne. No doubt disappointing the waitstaff (fifteen to twenty percent tip), I opt instead for the cheapest three-course fixed menu, one percent of the superburger's cost.

It is spring break, the week-long March holiday for North American college students, and roaming the sidewalks of the Strip at all hours are packs of young women and drunk, belligerent frat boys. If they have seemed over-testosteroned, later a biker gang checks into my hotel. Riding up in the elevator tonight with me are two cops.

"On level five we've got a guy who's decided to go outside on the balcony with no clothes on," one of them tells me. "Just another night in Vegas."

ARIZONA (BRIEFLY) AND NEW MEXICO

From Vegas the road winds out round the Hoover Dam. The barren expanse of Nevada is laid out before me and the semi-arid landscape continues crossing over into Arizona. As I pass by the Petrified Forest and Painted Desert strange rock formations catch the eye and mountains shaded with blue and purple line the horizon. Town names pass by like "Two Guns" and "Dead River". They can't compete with the best named place anywhere: Alberta, Canada's "Head Smashed-In Buffalo Jump".

The road is empty for whole stretches, giving the traveller the opportunity to re-imagine oneself as a cowboy roaming the Wild West, squinting into the sun and wondering where a bed might be made that night. Although, as this cowboy is carrying a credit card and sitting in an air-conditioned PT Cruiser, it's more like the Mild West. The countryside mellows for a while, sweeping pastoral panoramas, then turns bleakly red again entering into New Mexico.

Why is driving for long distances so much more enjoyable than being on a bus or train or plane? It's not that it's more comfortable. Perhaps it's the sense of being in control, able to stop and step out whenever you want. Or maybe it's just the feeling of being independent of schedule and timetables, other than the self-imposed.

In Albuquerque, set in the foothills of the Sandia Mountains, a cheap motel has cigarette burns on the sheets and rusted cars in the parking lot. Opposite is one of the two places in town I hit for New Mexican food the next day. Both have blue corn *enchiladas* with a choice of red or green chilli sauce (if you ask for "Christmas" you can get both) as well as the spicy pork stew *carne adovado*. New Mexican fare is a version of the American take on Mexican food that is also called Tex-Mex, Cal-Mex or Southwestern, depending on what state you find yourself in.

TEXAS

On into Texas, cattle and grain silos on the flat plains under brooding clouds. Signs flash by for Big Texas Ranch's 72-ounce steak (over 2 kilograms for the metric minded), free if you eat it all within one hour. That's the sort of thing that will help with the national obesity problem! Is it fair to see this obsession with quantity as a measure of quality, as particularly North American? When my US friends tell me about a new must-try burger place, it's often based on how big the burger was. You don't, after all, tend to see restaurants in Italy bragging about their all-you-can-eat spaghetti.

Renie & Sterling Steves look after me in Fort Worth, putting me up in the guest cottage behind the main house they have lived in for nearly fifty years. Sterling takes me on a tour of Fort Worth's historic districts, where real-life cowboys can be seen kicking back with a beer in the saloons. Renie, a cooking teacher and wine journalist, shows me round her enormous, jealousy-inducing cookbook library, which includes several she has authored.

One night we do a restaurant crawl, stopping at Lanny's Kitchen for appetisers before heading to Lonesome Dove for our mains. Renie takes me to lunch the next day at Kimbell Art Museum, where her friend Shelby runs the cafeteria, and afterwards I wander for a few hours around rooms of antiquities and the neighbouring building that runs more to the Modern.

A storm whips up heading south to Austin, some of the worst weather conditions of the entire trip. Rain slaps against the windshield as I pull in to Threadgill's, where Janis Joplin once propped up the bar. Chicken Fried Steak describes a steak fried like a chicken in the southern way. A tough cut of meat is pounded out thin to tenderise it, dipped in beaten egg and flour then plunged into oil to emerge crusty and browned. It's a less elegant descendant of the *schnitzel*, brought here by immigrants and adapted to the local ingredients. I relish every bite of Threadgill's, although am not as enamoured of country gravy, the bland, floury white sauce poured all over the steak and its mashed potatoes and beans. More of a brown gravy man, I am. Fork down, and moments later Austin is in the rear view mirror.

· · · · · · · · · ·

True Texas *Chili con carne* should not contain ground (minced) meat or beans, with even tomato optional. This is as defined by the late Francis X Tolbert, a newspaperman who did much to popularise Texas Chili and decry the sins committed in its name elsewhere. In old Grapevine, Texas, the restaurant Tolbert's, run by his daughter, is my stop for a "bowl of red" from his original recipe. It's one for the purists, although somewhat watery: finely-chopped lean beef cooked with chilli peppers and cumin, maybe a touch of beer added to the broth.

Southern Barbecue is a subject that could be a journey and a book in itself. The term barbecuing in much of the rest of the US (and world) means grilling over high temperature. Here in the southern states it refers to smoking meat for an extended period over indirect heat. Low and slow is the way to go. What animal and cut of meat is best, what sauce to use (if any), what combination of spices will yield the most succulent results - all are major points of contention to devotees. In Texas beef is king, as you go east to Tennessee and Carolina pork rules, and in Kentucky mutton gets a mention. The distinctions can get very precise for the connoisseur - Eastern North Carolinian barbecue, anyone?

In Texas a pilgrimage for revered barbecue means Dyer's in Amarillo and Sonny Bryan's shack in Dallas, which has dealt out popular 'cue for nearly a hundred years. Beef brisket and sausage are apparently the test of a barbecue joint in the Lone Star State, but at both places the brisket is kind of dry. However, back in Fort Worth Renie has her finger on the culinary pulse as always, and suggests for lunch Railhead BBQ. Their brisket is juicier, chopped or sliced into white bread sandwiches with pickles and a side of coleslaw and sauce.

American barbecue sauces range from clear (vinegar) and yellow (mustard-based) in the Carolinas, with minor forays into black (Worcestershire, Kentucky) and white (mayonnaise, Alabama), to tomato-heavy red throughout most of the South. In barbecue sauce, as in politics, Texas is a Red State. The red sauces are a bit sweet for me, tasting mostly of diluted ketchup.

ARKANSAS

When it comes to pancakes, there is the European model: lacy-thin crêpes, unleavened, best eaten rolled up with a sprinkling of sugar and a good squeeze of lemon juice. American pancakes are thicker, stauncher fare and can be stodgy. Fine for fortification if you were about to go toil in the frozen fields for hours, somewhat punishing otherwise.

But in Hot Springs in Arkansas my friend Sonya – the only person I know who keeps snakes as pets - takes me to breakfast at a local spot whose hotcakes are amazingly light and fluffy, and taste great smeared with butter and drenched in apricot syrup. Their texture is of an American pancake crossed with a British crumpet - some alchemy has gone into their making. Is it buttermilk for acidity, or club soda, or beaten egg whites folded into the mix? The server doesn't know, and isn't inclined to find out.

McClard's Bar-B-Q, our plan for dinner, is closed and our uninspiring alternative is Ruby Tuesday's, a QSR or Quick Service Restaurant. It becomes disheartening to roll through each new state and see the signs for the same nationwide chains over and over again. Boring, the quality usually low, and the death knell to mom-and-pop eateries squeezed out of business. People respond to familiar brands - it's a safe choice and they know what they're getting. Human nature, and I can't say too much, given my own fascination with those Vegas reproductions of restaurants from elsewhere.

LOUISIANA

The back roads from Arkansas across the border into Louisiana are a glimpse of small-town America: whiteboard houses, churches and battered gas stations, communities named "Hope" and "Plain Dealings". In Shreveport, Dorothy, who I last saw in India, offers a bed for the night. The family has an old cottage on the lake and her children are spending the day there. We drive down to it, magnolia trees dripping with Spanish moss and hornets buzzing about the eaves of the building. The kids have just seen a water moccasin, a large snake, swim by them in the water, and are duly excited. I am excited too, about the idea of not putting even a toe anywhere near that water.

We eat dinner at Superior Grill for good - if not superior - Tex-Mex food (and shouldn't it be Lou-Mex here?). Dorothy's husband Michael is a professional musician who plays in about five bands. We catch the end of one gig at a Shreveport casino and Dorothy persuades me to dance, a sight no civilized eye should have to see. People on the dance floor are averting their gaze in confusion at what is happening before them. Afterwards I help with loading the band gear and stay up until the wee hours with Michael and his vintage guitar collection and records of new sounds, to me at least: swamp rock, dark and blues based, and the accordion and washboard of zydeco.

Louisiana is one of the poorest states in the nation, further devastated recently by Hurricane Katrina. I drive east and south through communities made of mobile homes and boarded up shops. Drinking establishments aren't too inviting; windowless aluminium shacks with "BAR" or "NITECLUB" hand-scrawled on a door. "CASINOS" are more of the same - Vegas has nothing to worry about. Convicts in striped prisonwear collect trash by the roadside, watched over by their guards. But Southern mansions too are amidst the poverty, visions of faded glamour set back from the road.

Some of the most interesting food of the entire country is around these parts. Cajun cooking became trendy a few years back for a time, mostly thanks to chefs Paul Prudhomme and Emeril Lagasse, although by now 'Cajun' as a term has devolved outside Louisiana to indicate the presence of a bit of hot pepper. True Cajun and Creole cuisines have resulted from French, Spanish, African and southern US influences – France especially, via the Acadians of Canada. Many place and family names and cooking terms are French, and French is spoken in the older generations. Cajun could be summed up as the cooking of the countryside and Creole its more refined, aristocratic city cousin of New Orleans.

Both are intensely flavoured, many of the dishes prepared with the "Trinity" base of onion, celery and bell pepper, plus the cook's own proprietorial blend of spices and dried herbs. The thickening agent *roux*, fat and flour heated and stirred together until the colour of chocolate, gives rise to the local courting expression "Who's Your Mama, Are You Catholic, Can You Make a Roux?" It is a key to successfully making the thick soup *gumbo* (although there are roux-less versions thickened with okra or *filé* powder) and stews like *sauce piquante* and *etouffee*.

··········

I stop in Natchitoches for a meat pie at Lasyone's, plunked onto a plate with "dirty rice" cooked with chicken livers. In the afternoon it looks like it's going to be a fruitless hunt for *boudin* balls around the Acadiana district of Breaux Bridge and New Iberia. *Boudin* is a pork and rice sausage widely available in the area. Word is that some butchers and convenience stores slip the sausages out of their skins, form them into crackermeal-coated rounds and fry them up in lard.

Everywhere I try though they sell only regular steamed *boudin* or have run out of the balls. "Come early, come early!" is the continual refrain. I take solace in a brown paper bag of cracklins, spiced pork rinds, from the last butcher, and plan an early start the next day to track down the elusive balls.

There are no worries with getting up in the morning. Whoever had the room at the motel before has thoughtfully kept the clock radio alarm set at maximum volume for 5 am. By 7.30 Charlie J's butchery and general store has one remaining order left of three *boudin* balls. They are a bit like *arancini*, the rice balls Italians shape out of leftover risotto.

Regular *boudins* seem slightly familiar too. A distant cousin was over on the other side of the world, in Laos - the sour Lao sausage is also made with pork, rice and plenty of chilli heat. The Louisiana *boudins*, though, are much more loosely packed, and eaten by squeezing them out of their casings into the mouth. French influence was in Laos once as well as Louisiana - there could be some link between the sausages. (Sausage. Link. Another pun to file away and annoy people with later.)

Members of the McIlhenny family have made Tabasco sauce on Avery Island, near New Iberia, since 1863. The tour of their factory plant shows how ripe red capsicum peppers are aged with salt in oak barrels for up to three years, combined with vinegar and bottled and distributed around the world (I remember the miniature bottles that came with the army packs of US peacekeepers in Cambodia to enliven their rations). These days many of the peppers for the sauce are grown in South and Central America.

After lunch at Victor's Cafeteria in New Iberia (chosen because that's where the fictional detective Dave Robicheaux eats) I head on the 10 East freeway through the Louisiana wetlands, the marsh on either side of the highway speckled with swamp trees, and by late afternoon am in Jackson, Mississippi.

MISSISSIPPI

Greenwood is a town in the Mississippi Delta north of Jackson. Here my friends Carol and Leanne live and work for the Viking Range Corporation, manufacturers of stovetops for home and professional kitchens.

Accents are getting real Southern by now. "Yes" is now "Yee-uss". The trouble understanding people goes both ways - at least one waiter is convinced English isn't my native language and becomes extra loud and slow. People are especially polite in this part of the country - "Hey, how you doin'?" as you pass a stranger on the street - and locals introduce themselves with both first and last name.

Carol and Leanne are members of the Southern Foodways Alliance, a collection of chefs, writers and academics dedicated to documenting and celebrating "the diverse food cultures of the American South". Their annual symposiums are four days of animated discussions and demonstrations, interspersed with snacks of pig ears and Coca Colas laced with salted peanuts. (At one of the symposiums I once cornered Allan Benton of chef favourite Benton's Hams. I thought he was riveted in what I had to say until the slightest flicker of his face made me suddenly realize that, as a Southerner, he was merely being well-mannered - I quickly wrapped the conversation up.)

It's all very akin to the philosophy of the Slow Food movement, and in fact Carol's a Slow Fooder as well. She arranges for me to stay at the Alluvian, a boutique hotel across the road from the Viking headquarters. Bowls of apples and fine artworks line the corridors, the soft, comfortable bed a change from dodgy motel mattresses. Grits are available one morning in the breakfast room, a southern staple of cornmeal porridge similar to Italian polenta and (like polenta) best enjoyed when well buttered.

Greenwood is so preserved it almost looks like a film set, like a Hollywood producer's idea of a Depression era country town. A church on the outskirts holds the grave of bluesman Robert Johnson (one of three grave sites claiming him), who as legend has it sold his soul to the devil at the crossroads. Carol and I clear away the empty liquor bottles around the tombstone but leave the harmonica someone has placed there.

Lusco's was opened in 1933 by Italian immigrants and is the most old-fashioned spot, living history. The dining room is made up of curtained booths for privacy (and back during Prohibition, shielded prying eyes from a little imbibing). To summon the server you push a buzzer. The menu of simple steaks and seafood has a fairly recently added - and singular - choice of "Vegetable". It was a tradition for generations of drunken Greenwoodites to flick pats of butter onto the ceiling, creating a rancid paste which when the weather warmed would drip down onto future diners. The ceiling has been scoured clean now, and these days the butter comes in sealed little tubs.

An hour southwest of Greenwood through the cotton fields is Greenville and Doe's Eat Place, a family restaurant and former grocery store from the 1940's. Inside the wooden house the kitchen is set in the middle of the dining room, taking the idea of open kitchens to a whole other level. Steaks, charred outside while pinkly juicy within, sizzle under the hot broiler near the entrance. The contents of cast iron skillets, further blackened with age and use, splutter on top of the ancient range surrounded by patrons. Doe's has won the James Beard Award for Classic Restaurant this year, and owner Barbara gets to make her first ever trip to New York next month for the ceremony.

· · · · · · · · · ·

Fried chicken has universal appeal, but the representation of Southern fried chicken that is known worldwide is the cheap, factory-raised poultry parts of a certain three-letter acronym (Corporate Chain Chicken?). Those parts are encased in a grease-sodden breading which supposedly contains a secret blend of herbs and spices, but which has been analysed in the past to find only salt (and lots of it), pepper and monosodium glutamate. It's not the greatest ambassador for one of the glories of Southern cooking (although a guilty pleasure, there's something perversely appealing about that gelatinous crust).

My goal while in the Deep South is to learn how good fried chicken can really be, when prepared with care and respect by skilful cooks. That starts in Greenwood, as Leanne takes me to lunch at Crystal Grill.

Carol has described their fried chicken as "serious", and it is. Flakes of the spring bird's lightly crunchy, well-seasoned batter give way to moist breast meat. Rice and turnip greens with pepper vinegar round out the plate, with sweetened ice tea, "the house wine of the South", to drink.

Hot tamales on the menu are a legacy of Hispanic labourers in the area in the early 20th century. I have no room for dessert but it is necessary, purely out of politeness of course, to partake of a couple of wedges of the Grill's famous pies, lemon icebox and Mile-High Coconut Cream topped with a sweet cloud of meringue.

TENNESSEE

Mason is a hamlet not far out of Memphis, known foremost for Gus' World Famous Fried Chicken. Reviews say people are usually lining out the door, but I am early enough to be the only customer.

The remarkable thing about Gus' chicken is how greaseless it is. Like the best Japanese *tempura*, it's been cooked at exactly the right temperature for the hot oil to create a crisp shell around the pieces and not penetrate the interior (unlike Corporate Chain Chicken!) It has a nicely spicy kick too, the battered crust reddish from cayenne pepper or hot sauce. On the other hand, compared to Crystal Grill, Gus' bird is way saltier, and the white breast meat has dried out.

Across the road stands another Mason landmark, Bozo's Barbecue. I walk over afterwards for a 'cue sandwich in the Memphis manner: mushy white bread slices around chopped pork shoulder, coleslaw and, this being Tennessee, red sauce.

Hamburgers rival fried chicken and barbecue for icon status in the US. Regional variations abound. I once went in search of the steamed cheeseburger, native of mid Connecticut, the meat an unappetising grey instead of brown but delicious and brimming with juice.

The other end of the spectrum from steaming a burger must be to deep-fry it, and that's what Dyer's in Memphis do, poaching their patties in rendered beef dripping they claim to have reused for over nine decades. Trying one, once, may be enough.

GEORGIA

The fried chicken adventure continues the next night at dinner at Watershed in Decatur. Here they meticulously transform the chicken, a Tuesday night special only. The pieces are soaked in saltwater, bathed in buttermilk, floured and shallow-fried in a combination of butter and ham-infused lard. Carol and Leanne have alerted Watershed's chef, also a member of Southern Foodways Alliance, to my impending arrival.

"I believe you are travelling around the world!" says the server, and brings a complimentary soup and appetiser.

The meals of the following days blur together: "meat & three" (vegetables, that is) at Wilson's Soul Food in Athens; a chilli slaw dog and pimento cheeseburger at student hangout The Varsity, also in Athens; more fried chicken in Atlanta at Son's Place and Southern fine dining at Eugene's. Some pink Pepto-Bismol antacid is in there somewhere.

The weather has a chill to it and I miss my jacket, left back in an Alabama motel. I witness a lot of waste in my travels. Large quantities of untouched food sit on tables and will end up discarded, while just outside the front doors many will be going hungry. Some cooks are taking notice too. At one restaurant I visit they start completely from scratch every morning, and give everything made the day before and uneaten away to the homeless.

The difference between "soul" and "Southern US" food isn't clear to me, other than that the term "soul food" will probably designate that the food was made by an African-American cook. The dishes are much the same in the South at both black and white establishments. Venues range from the modest (Martha Lou's two-booth shack in Charleston, South Carolina) to the grand (Mary Mac's Tea Room in

Atlanta), and the communal tables of Mrs Wilke's boarding house in Savannah, Georgia.

At Mrs Wilke's, dishes are placed family-style in the middle of each table and passed around by the diners. Mains are meatloaf, fried chicken and pork chops, but it's the vegetable preparations that are the most interesting: lima beans, sweet potatoes, black-eyed peas, okra with tomatoes, candied yams, pickled beets and collard greens. *Potlikker*, the liquid exuded from the long cooked greens, comes with cornbread for dunking. Another plate holds biscuits, which in the UK or Australia would be "scones". If one didn't eat meat one could make a fine feast out of Southern vegetable dishes, although many are cooked with a bit of animal fat to flavour them.

INDIANA

Leaving the South up the interstate freeways, winds buffeting the car, in Indianapolis I turn into the parking lot of Shapiro's, a Jewish delicatessen that dates back to 1905.

A signature of the US Jewish deli experience, other than rude waiters, is "Pastrami on Rye". Seeded rye bread, spread with mustard, is heaped high with steamed, thinly-sliced pink meat. Pastrami, smoked cured beef, is probably a New World child of the Turkish/Armenian *basturma* (although *basturma*'s strong-on-the-fenugreek spice rub has been replaced by an emphasis on coriander and black pepper). A sour dill pickle on the side counterpoints the greasiness of the sandwich.

Shapiro's version is OK, but it can't hold a candle (or dill pickle) to the overstuffed sandwiches at delis like Katz's in New York. The waiters aren't gruff enough either.

MICHIGAN

It's April, but this morning my windshield is iced over and patches of snow are on the ground. Zingerman's Roadhouse in Ann Arbor provides a speedy way to warm up with high-quality, respectful renditions of classics from all over the US. Think macaroni and cheese but made with raw milk Vermont cheddar and artisanal Italian durum pasta. The peppered bacon rashers from Arkansas are pretty formidable too. Zingerman's is an edible tour around the country, all under one roof. I could have just eaten here and saved on all that gasoline.

IOWA

Monday and Tuesday I drive over a thousand miles for two sandwiches. First I barrel across the expanses of the Midwestern plains to Marshalltown, Iowa, home of Taylor's Maid-Rite. Taylor's are renowned for their "loosemeat" sandwich, an Iowan creation of a generic bun filled with crumbled ground beef, chopped raw onion, mustard and dill pickle. Looking like a disintegrated hamburger or a Sloppy Joe without the sauce, it comes with a teaspoon, as there's no way to eat all of it without spilling the filling.

Maid-Rite is now a franchised chain throughout the Midwest, but Taylor's has stood fast on a number of principles, refusing, for example, to compromise by using headquarters' precooked, vacuum-packed meat. Instead, they grind their own beef in-store from select cattle. You have to support the little guy who insists on doing it the old-fashioned, more labour-and-cost-intensive way to ensure better quality. When the staff at Taylor's enquire after my accent, and hear how far I have travelled that morning to visit them, they are duly impressed and press a second sandwich I don't really need upon me.

KANSAS

Jumping back into the car - or to be more accurate, after two sandwiches and a malt shake, gingerly lowering myself in behind the wheel - it's south to Kansas City, sharing the road with freight trucks and giant RVs. Local radio offers a choice of country music or Christian stations, or Christian country music stations.

By now I've put away several kinds of US barbecue, my personal preference so far the sauceless "dry rub" ribs of Memphis sheathed in a bark of spices. To tick the last of the major barbecue boxes requires Kansas City barbecue, and I draw up to Arthur Bryant's just as dusk is setting in. My "burnt ends" sandwich is chopped bits of blackened brisket slathered with a thick, spicy tomato sauce. The sandwich is a great one - primal and satisfying. Bryant's barbecue sauce is not as ketchupy as most others; sweet enough but not as sugar laden and more about the vinegar.

ILLINOIS

Now I'm in a city where the L-train rattles overhead. The urban downtown makes one think of Manhattan and the funky suburbs of Toronto. Joggers run along Chicago's lakeshore, although at this time of year no-one is venturing into the choppy waves. At breakfast at Lou Mitchell's I take issue with their corned beef hash, which is described as "homemade" on the menu but is straight out of a tin.

"But we warmed it up!" protests the server.

Chicago is at the forefront of the fledgling modernist cuisine movement in North America. I make it to Moto's for a twenty-course and nearly four-hour meal that might be even more over the top than Britain's Fat Duck and Spain's El Bulli Hotel. A forerunner of what's to come is the menu itself - it turns out to be the first course, edible food dye printed onto a cracker.

Some of the standouts of this "post-modern" meal include pasta made out of gelled lychee juice and savoury ice creams. Pancakes are made tableside by ejecting batter from a syringe onto a "chill grill" with the cold steel doing the "cooking" (tuna cubes also get this reverse grilling treatment). Halfway through the meal, the waiter gives me a pair of safety goggles and escorts me downstairs for a tour of the kitchen-as-lab, where lasers and canisters of liquid nitrogen share space with the more traditional whisks and pans of the trade. One day this sort of thing may seem as dated as the worst excesses of 1970s nouvelle cuisine, but right now it feels fun and cutting edge.

··········

This is a town obsessed with hot dogs, and it takes a couple of days to get around to some of the famous, or infamous, stands that sell them. The wiener isn't taken lightly in Illinois. A Chicago "red hot" will add to its frankfurter and poppy seed bun any or all of the following: yellow mustard, luridly green relish, raw or grilled onion, slices of tomato and cucumber, dill pickle and bell peppers, the whole to be sprinkled with celery salt.

By the time all this vertical salad has been piled on there's no longer any sight of the dog itself. How this particular combination came to be canonical is a mystery, and it seems impossible to eat one where the bun doesn't disintegrate after a couple of bites into a tasty container of bread stew, from the weight of all the toppings.

Doug Sohn is a culinary school graduate who at "Hot Doug's" has brought a chef's sensibility to the hot dog. A "Teuben" is a play on the classic Reuben deli sandwich, here a corned beef hot dog topped with melted Swiss cheese and caraway-laced sauerkraut. His Chicago red hot is traditional and impeccable. A duck *confit* dog is daubed with black truffle butter.

The duck dog is a little dry, as it doesn't have its usual ingredient of foie gras added in. Doug Sohn and leading Chicago chefs Rick Tramonto and Charlie Trotter have all been embroiled in the recent controversy over the recent banning by the city of Chicago of foie gras (force-fed geese or ducks liver fattened up to ten times normal size).

Tramonto and Trotter have been in opposite corners. Trotter is one of the key figures denouncing the production of foie gras as cruel, while Tramonto defends the right of restaurants to serve it and customers to choose it or not. Meanwhile Sohn had been continuing to sell it at Hot Doug's in defiance of the ban, but was recently taken to court and fined. During a short taxi ride to get to Hot Doug's a brief debate starts – initiated by the cabbie, who knows of the story - over whether I should even eat there.

NEW YORK

In the delis of Brooklyn's Jewish neighbourhoods the regulars nosh away under a barrage of affectionate - I think - insults from the owners. (I write down some of the more hilarious insults, but lose the piece of paper afterwards.) Hasidic Jews live in a close-knit community here, the boys in pigtails and dressed in black clothes and hats, the men the same but with full beards. For block after block they are almost all one sees on the sidewalks until at Broadway Avenue they abruptly end, at the border of their world.

It's hard to imagine that in just a few weeks the streets of Manhattan will be filled with shorts and T-shirts as summer sets in, the weather warms and the light begins to linger in the evenings. For now people are still in overcoats, scarves and bulky clothing.

At a chef's conference in lower Manhattan the hottest chefs from Spain and the leading US "modernist cuisine" exponents demonstrate their recent findings. The ideas really are getting out there - the Spanish are exploring the concept of compost infusions, and of flavours of clay, dirt and soil. A Japanese chef uses a hospital-grade CT scanner to work out how to cut up his fish.

I notice a real generational divide - the old school French and Italian chefs think taste and texture are being sacrificed to technique by the modernists. The young Turks - or here, rather, Spaniards/Americans – show respect but some, privately, dismiss their concerns as those of boring old has-beens. The way it has always been and always will be.

··········

I have driven right across this vast country, from San Francisco till the road ran out at Savannah, then back again halfway to Chicago and up across to the east coast. In New York we've reached the end of the journey, at least for now. And the end of this book. And the end, alas, to what had been, before the trip, a healthy bank balance.

We should finish with something sweet. Doughnuts.

There's never been a better time to be a doughnut lover in New York. Artisan bakers and some of the city's finest chefs have been turning their talents to reworking and refining the fried pastries.

The main choice is between yeast raised doughnuts and the cake kind, leavened with baking powder. The epitome of the yeast experience is those made from brioche dough. They are appearing increasingly on menus here, the *crème brulée* of the mid noughties. One of the richest doughs imaginable - up to seven eggs and three quarters of a pound of butter to three cups flour! - is deep-fried and stuffed with citrus curd or pastry cream, more full fat dairy and eggs. You wonder if they should be labelled with a surgeon general's warning, although by then you are on your third.

Where are the city's best? Not at Thomas Keller's Bouchon Bakery or Mark Israel's Doughnut Plant in the Lower East Side. Carefully made with imagination and fine ingredients, these fall short of greatness simply because they aren't served hot and fresh. The magic of doughnuts ebbs each second they are away from the oil – they should no more be relished cold than French fries. Hopefully, I rap on the glass of Bouchon's darkened doorway early on a Saturday morning, but the bakers toiling away in the back tell me to come back in three hours when the store officially opens.

The advantage goes to restaurants, then, who will cook them to order. One is truly spoilt for choice. The Italian *bomboloni* of A Voce and Insieme and the buttermilk *beignets* with plum compote at Cookshop meet more eccentric offerings like Riingo's green tea doughnuts and the curry *pan* at Morimoto. The downside of all this bounty is the need to factor in the considerable cost of an entire meal to get to it. Signs, however, are encouraging – NYC celebrity cooks can't stop opening casual burger shacks and upscale sandwich shops. Can their reboots on Krispy Kreme be far away?

To ensure my cake-style doughnuts are warm I drive the hundred miles from Manhattan to Scoop Du Jour in East Hampton, trying to time traffic to turn up at the same moment as a new batch. "We make them every couple of hours," says the girl by the counter.

No instant gratification on arrival, but the reward of waiting is a narrative in grease; extruded rings of batter set sail through seething fat, climb valiantly up a conveyor belt and free fall into a dredging of spiced sugar. Eaten the moment I can pick one up without burning my fingers, they are a paean to tradition.

Back in the Big Apple at the new Primehouse on Park Avenue, if there's still stomach room after dry-aged beef and skillets of hash browns the "Box Of Doughnuts" arrives tableside, with three miniature squeeze bottles of fillings for you to play pastry chef. Perfectly fried, the little balls are dry to the touch with fluffy, pale yellow interiors. A block away at Pamplona the modern tapas menu concludes with *bunuelos* – mini doughnut holes with bittersweet cocoa added and liquid ganache inside ready to ooze out. What's not to love about a dessert that's a confluence of doughnut, brownie and one of those molten-centred chocolate cakes?

What would I call my own boutique doughnut shop, if I had one? I decide on "Glazed and Confused". And I could hand out 'frequent fryer' cards to customers. . . But what a lot of work it would be, in order to rise above the mediocre. Better in this case, perhaps, to be a consumer than creator.

Brioche or baking powder? Pillowy squishiness and the taste of sweet bread, or the reassuring density of cake? I pause, smile at my good fortune to live in a Renaissance Age of the doughnut, and plan on both. As long as they're hot.

ETOUFFEE

There's nothing refined about this highly-seasoned stew – it's a rustic taste of rural Louisiana. Really it should be made with Cajun andouille sausage, but good luck finding that outside of Louisiana or major US cities. I usually substitute chorizo, but kielbasa or another firm smoked pork sausage would also work.

A Cajun cook might object – among other things! – to the presence of tomato paste here, considering that more a cityfied Creole touch. Nor are coriander and cumin traditional, but I like how they round out the spice blend. You do whatever lets you sleep at night.

It's essential to have the ingredients chopped, measured out and ready beforehand, since once the process starts you are pretty much standing at the stove stirring.

Serve over steamed white rice (a Cajun way is to invert a cup of rice into each person's bowl and then ladle the stew around it).

Spice mix:

1½ teaspoons sweet paprika (preferably Hungarian)

1 teaspoon salt

½ teaspoon cayenne pepper

½ teaspoon freshly ground black pepper,

Heaped ½ teaspoon ground coriander (optional)

Scant ½ teaspoon ground cumin (optional)

¼ cup (60 ml) canola or vegetable oil

⅓ cup flour

1 medium brown onion, very finely chopped

2 celery stalks, very finely chopped

1 green bell pepper/capsicum, very finely chopped

2 cloves garlic, minced

100 g (3½ ounces) andouille, chorizo or other smoked pork
sausage, halved lengthways then sliced crosswise into half discs

1 tablespoon tomato paste

4 boneless skinless chicken thighs,
about 500 g (1.1 pounds) total, cut into 4cm (1½ inch) chunks

½ teaspoon additional freshly ground black pepper

2 tablespoons flat-leaf parsley, chopped

1 tablespoon freshly squeezed lemon juice (about ¼ lemon)
plus additional to taste

Combine spice mix ingredients in a small bowl. Heat the oil in a heavy-bottomed, medium saucepan over medium heat. Add the flour and cook, stirring constantly with a wooden spoon, until the roux is a dark peanut butter colour, almost the colour of milk chocolate. (Depending on pot, stove and heat source this has taken me anywhere from 15 to 45 minutes.) Be very careful not to splash the roux on bare skin – there's a reason it's also called "Cajun Napalm"!

Immediately add the onion, celery and green pepper and cook, stirring often, until vegetables are very soft and wilted, about 15 minutes.

Add the garlic and cook 3 minutes, then the sausage and cook 2 minutes. Stir in the spice mix and cook 1 minute, then add tomato paste and cook for 5 minutes.

Now add the chicken and turn it around in the mixture, then add 1 cup (250 ml) water. Raise heat to bring to a boil, reduce heat to medium low and simmer covered, occasionally stirring the bottom and skimming off any excess oil and scum from the surface, until the chicken is tender (a knife blade pierces through without resistance) in a thick gravy, about 30 minutes. If the gravy is too thin, simmer uncovered until it reduces to the right consistency.

Add the black pepper and cook for another 5 minutes. Turn off heat, let sit for a couple of minutes then skim off any excess oil from surface and add the parsley and lemon juice. Taste and see if more salt or lemon juice is needed.

You can eat now, or it's good to let it rest overnight in the fridge and then reheat.

APPENDIX

STOCK

You can use store-bought stock in the recipes, and I do sometimes, but they are often not flavourful enough or too salty – or both! – so it's not the same as making your own. Making stock takes time but not much effort, and you could make a large batch and store in the freezer in recipe-sized portions for up to 3 months.

Adding one or two veal knucklebones or a split pig's trotter along with the chicken will add body to the stock.

I use chicken wings here but you can use any chicken parts. The meat and bones should be cut into small pieces to release their flavour into the liquid.

Approximate cooking time: 3 hours

2 kgs (4½ pounds) chicken wings

1 large onion, cut into chunks

Place the onion in a large pot and top with the chicken pieces. Cover with cold water, bring to a boil and skim off the scum and froth from the surface. Reduce heat to low and simmer gently uncovered, just a few lazy bubbles, for 2½ hours, skimming occasionally.

Taste the stock. If it is still watery, continue to cook until it has a nice light 'chicken soup' flavour. Strain though a fine-mesh strainer into a large bowl or container. Cool quickly and refrigerate. (Discard the solids or you can eat them, but the chicken has given its all to the stock and will be dry and tasteless.)

The next day, remove the congealed fat from the surface and discard. If the stock has set into a jelly that is a good sign and means it has lots of body. Store the stock for up to 3 days in the refrigerator, or freeze in individual half-cup or one-cup portions for up to 3 months.